The 3 Personalities
of Money

The 3 Personalities of Money

A Breakthrough Discovery In
"Mind over Money"

Tony Walker

authorHOUSE®

AuthorHouse™
1663 Liberty Drive
Bloomington, IN 47403
www.authorhouse.com
Phone: 1-800-839-8640

Published by AuthorHouse   03/12/2013

ISBN: 978-1-4817-1824-0 (sc)
ISBN: 978-1-4817-1828-8 (e)

Library of Congress Control Number: 2013903136

The material contained in this book is for general information purposes only. It does not constitute legal advice, tax advice, investment advice, or other advice, nor is it intended to recommend any particular investments, products, or financial instruments. The content herein and the concept of The 3 Personalities of Money* *Financial Profile represent the views and opinions of the author. Information contained in this book should not be used as the basis for decisions regarding the purchase or sale of any investment. Always seek advice from your financial advisor, attorney, or accountant with regard to investment, legal, or tax questions.*

"WorryFree Retirement, The 3 Personalities of Money and Mailbox Money are registered trademarks of Walker Financial Services, Inc."

Contents

Preface

Just as no two snowflakes are alike, no two people are either. We each have a personality that we show the world, which is unique in its own way to each one of us. Our friends, family members, bosses, coworkers, neighbors, acquaintances, and even the kid who hands the coffee to us each morning can rattle off characteristics we display. But what we reveal to one may not be what we reveal to another. We show different people different aspects of ourselves, and there's always more to us than what others see.

Can our personalities be completely defined by a list of traits? I don't think so. The whole is greater than the sum of the parts. Our personalities are made up of physical, mental, emotional, and spiritual components. They're molded and colored and given intricacies by our upbringing, our experiences, our fears, our passions, and our observations of the world; this is true even when it comes to how we think, feel, and act regarding money.

So here's how I really am going to change your life! *The 3 Personalities of Money* lets you discover how you're wired financially. By the time you finish this little book, you'll know more about this important truth and will gain a better understanding of the financial products and financial strategies that best suit you—when to take social security and whether to "max out" your 401(k), to name a few financial decisions you may need to make. Armed with this new information, you will be better prepared to pick investment strategies that leave you feeling comfortable, and confident, and not second-guessing yourself. You'll stop following the herd, investing and saving in particular ways just because it seems to be what everyone else is doing. And you'll definitely embrace your newly found worry-free financial life, living by the principles of *mind over money* (my approach), rather than *money over mind* (the financial world's approach).

Once you affirm your financial personality, I'll guide you on how best to utilize this newfound self-knowledge to make the right decisions *for you* without getting lost in the endless advice, questionnaires, guilt trips, and ulterior motives spun by others.

Your financial personality is just one aspect of who you are. *The 3 Personalities of Money* is not intended to pigeonhole or oversimplify anyone. I don't claim that I can define you. I don't pretend, like so many out there, to have some secret knowledge or magic financial bullet that will always target what is best for you.

What I have here are, to some extent, generalizations. There's no way around that when you're writing a book for everyone. After you finish reading, head over to 3Personalities.com and take the free 3-minute test so you can quickly determine your financial personality.

The stories located at the end of this book will get you thinking about your options and opinions on a whole host of real-world financial situations. All of this is the result of my background in psychology, decades of experience in the financial trenches with all sorts of people, expert consultations, lots of interviews with lots of different folks, and a drive to understand why people do what they do with their money.

The 3 Personalities of Money is your guide. I want to help you figure out how you're wired financially, so you aren't even slightly tempted by the people out there pretending they have secret knowledge about you and where you should be investing your money.

Only you can make the right choices for your life. Only you can define yourself.

Upon completing this book, which is simply an introduction to this new and exciting concept, and after taking the free 3 Personalities of Money test, you'll begin the exciting journey toward a better understanding of which financial products and strategies are right for you—which ones are most comfortable and most suited to your unique financial makeup. And isn't that what having money is all about—to use and enjoy it with the least amount of worry? I think so. In fact, after working with thousands of people, I know so.

The mission of my life's work in the field of money and people is helping others worry less about both. I trust you will discover, as I have, that when it comes to money, there is one simple truth we can all live by: It's not about the money, but about knowing who we are and what we want out of life.

We have little control over global economic trends, currency fluctuations and devaluations, natural disasters, political upheavals, social unrest, bad weather, or schizophrenic stock markets. We do, however, have complete control over our own behavior, an accountability we relish.

—Excerpt from Coca-Cola's 1994 report by former CEO Roberto Goizueta, as provided by Nikki Ross, in her book Lessons from the Legends of Wall Street

CHAPTER 1

The 3 Personalities of Money

. . . a breakthrough concept in
"Mind over Money"

Here are three words that my granddad lived by:
"Never borrow money."

Then again, here are—hold on, let me count
them—*eight* words that an investor friend of mine
lives by: *"Borrowing money is one way to grow
money."*

On the other hand, I know a high roller from
Vegas who lives by these *nine* words: *"Borrowing
money is the only way to grow money."*

Three different people, three different
answers—how can this be?

"Different strokes for different folks," you say.

I think there's more to it than that. Let me
show you what I mean. Quickly take 60 seconds to

answer *agree* or *disagree* to the following financial questions. Go ahead; I'll wait.

1. Paying off your home mortgage as quickly as possible is always best. *Agree/Disagree*
2. Paying off your home mortgage early is bad, since interest rates are low now, giving you more opportunities to invest your money for higher returns. *Agree/Disagree*
3. Maxing out your 401(k) is something everyone should do, since it reduces taxes. *Agree/Disagree*
4. Maxing out your 401(k) may be a lousy idea, because there is a the lack of investment options right now and you will still owe future taxes when you retire. *Agree/Disagree*
5. Compound interest is a wonderful concept. *Agree/Disagree*
6. Compound interest is a nightmare, since you are paying taxes on the same dollar more than once. *Agree/Disagree*
7. Buying term life insurance is the best way to purchase life insurance, since it is so cheap. *Agree/Disagree*
8. Buying term life insurance only makes the insurance companies rich, as most people never die during the term of the policy. *Agree/Disagree*
9. Investing in fixed annuities is a great way to guarantee income for life. *Agree/Disagree*

10. Investing in fixed annuities is too restrictive and won't keep pace with inflation. *Agree/ Disagree*

So now you have your answers, correct?

Now, what if I randomly asked over 100 people from a wide variety of backgrounds and experience the same questions? (I've already done this in much more detail by hiring psychologists in the field to create an accurate way to measure this, as you will see in a minute.) Do you think they'd come up with exactly the same answers as you did?

Of course not!

Before we get too far into why this is true and the subject matter of *The 3 Personalities of Money,* I must confess that when it comes to my views on money, some in the financial world might consider me a weird bird. That's because I'm one of the few financial advisors in the country possessing a formal education and experience in both psychology and finance. The longer I'm in this field, the more I believe an advisor should possess (some) skills in both fields of psychology (the how and why we form our impressions and perceptions of the world and our behavior) and in the field of money (where to invest our money based on the understanding of who we are). When you consider that both are components in the planning process, why shouldn't advisors have credentials in both?

By the way, while it is true that I majored in psychology and continue to study a great deal on the subject of psychology, I don't pretend to be an expert—I'm not a psychologist. Yet that doesn't stop my wife, Susan, who, knowing I've always had an interest in the mystery of why we dream (in college, I was captivated by Carl Jung's work Memories, Dreams, and Reflections*), from constantly asking me to interpret her dreams. She'll routinely wake up to inform me of a previous night's dream and then ask for my interpretation. She always gets the same response: "Honey, I have no idea."*

Today's consumers are dazed and confused for good reason. I witness their frustrations in my daily practice, in financial workshops, and I hear it from them each week during my weekly call-in show on television. Over the past 30 years, I have spoken with thousands of people about their money. And here's the reason for much of their confusion: They are listening to a financial world whose *only* perspective is money.

No one would argue that an understanding of money and economics is crucial to making wise financial decisions, but the financial world lacks understanding, thus avoiding one of the most powerful components in the money decision process—personality. What has developed are two camps of advisors (schools of thought, if you will); the Old School, which has always focused on the money side of things, and a new breed of advisors and academics, who attempt to flank the other side as they bring the element of psychology to the table—the "behavioral" side. Both sides are valid; however, neither side has figured out how to mold the two schools of thought together. Just read all of their studies and you'll quickly discover that the two camps are not on the same page.

The 3 Personalities of Money solves this mystery. It merges the two schools of thought into one. That's because they should have never been separated in the first place. You can't explain your money decisions without first knowing yourself.

After personal study and experience spanning four different decades of working with money and people, I've come to the conclusion that this is not complicated. When you boil it down to the basics, each of us possesses one of three predominant financial personalities—a person is either a *saver, investor*, or *speculator.* That's it. One of these will be the predominant driver behind your financial thinking and subsequent decisions. We'll learn a lot more about them soon.

Why does each of us possess such a personality? Hard to say, but I feel it is a combination of nature/nurture. We are born hard-wired a certain way by nature and we also are affected by our upbringing and experiences—nurture's effect on our development. If you have children (my wife and I have three), I'm sure you agree that while each popped out of the same hatch, they may have totally different personalities from one another. When it comes to money, my kids all handle money

Risk Tolerance Analysis

No.	Question	Response
1	I seek a higher-than-average growth rate in the value of my portfolio and am willing to accept greater investment risk to do so.	2
2	I want to assure that I am protected against the erosion of the future purchasing power of my investment assets due to inflation.	2
3	I want to minimize my current taxes by shifting my tax burden to later years.	2
4	My investments do not need to generate a high level of spendable income (dividends & interest).	2
5	I would characterize my investment objectives and outlook as long-term in nature (over 7 years). I am not concerned about the short-term.	2
6	I would be willing to tolerate more volatility and the risk of short-term loss in my investment portfolio in order to achieve a higher expected return.	2
7	I do not need to readily convert my investment assets into cash. I have other liquid assets to meet any major emergency expenditures.	2
8	Given historical returns on different kinds of investments, my desired level of investment return is above-average.	2
9	I am willing to bear an above-average level of investment risk. I can accept occasional years with negative investment returns.	2
10	Barring unforeseen circumstances, I expect to need this money _____ years from now. (Divide answer by 2).	2

Responses: 1 = Strongly Disagree; 5 = Strongly Agree

Your Risk Profile: Conservative

Use of risk tolerance analysis is one approach for helping you select a suitable portfolio. Your risk profile has been determined based on your responses to the risk questionnaire. This information was used to identify a range of portfolios on the Efficient Frontier that one considers appropriate for your risk profile.

January 13, 1998

Figure 1.1 Sample Risk Tolerance Questionnaire and responses.

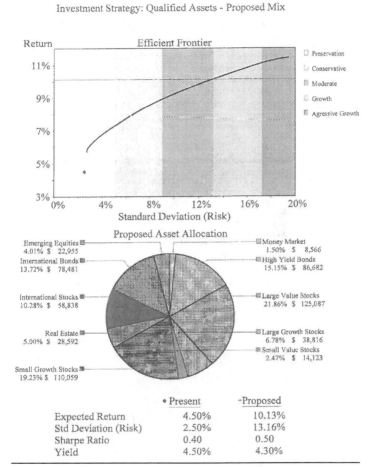

Investment Strategy: Qualified Assets - Proposed Mix

January 9, 1998

Figure 1.2—Asset Allocation diagram following completion of risk tolerance questionnaire.

A word of caution: the financial world hates simple and loves complicated. Here's why: The more complicated they can make the world of money, the more likely you are to rely on them to guide you. The Bible's Golden Rule says, "Do unto others as you would have others do unto you." Meantime, the Golden Rule of the financial world is, "He who makes the rules gets the gold." The game of money is about who controls it. The financial world (which includes our friends in Washington cranking out rules day and night while borrowing from the Fed like there's no tomorrow) makes money on other people's money (OPM). That's what they do, and they are darn good at it. It is that simple. If they successfully make the information complicated, you'll stay confused and fearful and thus continue to hand your money over to them for them to control. Keeping you confused and in the dark is their game plan. *The 3 Personalities of Money* will put a stop to their tactics by putting you in control of your money.

There's no reason to make this stuff so complicated. As far back as the mid-1990s, I was using technology to report my clients' securities accounts, all on one simple page. I've attached one of the actual reports (Figure 1.3), dated 1997, that I randomly dug up from my practice. As far back as 1997, we had the ability to illustrate the actual rate of return (even after my fee was deducted) for any period of time! In this case, it was from 7-8-97 thru 7-15-97, a random seven-day period of time selected for some reason by our client. No 20-page report from Wall Street with meaningless numbers scattered throughout; notice that our entire client's portfolio of investments and actual performance and fees is all on just one page! And this was over 15 years ago, before the latest, greatest technology of today. So why in the world doesn't the financial world make it this simple? The answer: Making things complicated keeps them in control and keeps you hanging on for dear life.

Tony Walker

Walker Financial Services
PERFORMANCE BY SECURITY

From 07-08-97 To 07-15-97

Security	Average Capital	Realized Gains	Unrealized Gains	Interest Dividends	IRR -Fees	07-15-97 Market Value	Pct. of Assets
MUTUAL FUNDS							
Amer Cent Benham European Govt Bond	27,861.00	0.00	(610.10)	0.00	(2.19)	27,250.90	6.24
BT Investment International Equity	23,518.00	0.00	(119.38)	0.00	(0.51)	23,398.62	5.36
Babson Value	45,265.00	0.00	443.06	0.00	0.98	45,708.06	10.46
Baron Asset	28,403.00	0.00	814.78	0.00	2.87	29,217.78	6.69
Cohen & Steers Realty Shares	21,688.00	0.00	340.44	0.00	1.57	22,028.44	5.04
Dreyfus Appreciation	29,610.00	0.00	459.44	0.00	1.55	30,069.44	6.88
Federated High-Yield	32,877.00	0.00	104.48	0.00	0.32	32,981.48	7.55
Federated International Income A	27,861.00	0.00	(515.47)	0.00	(1.85)	27,345.53	6.26
Kemper High Yield	32,877.00	0.00	117.28	0.00	0.36	32,994.28	7.55
Managers International Equity	23,518.00	0.00	(176.81)	0.00	(0.75)	23,341.19	5.34
Montgomery Emerging Markets	8,637.00	0.00	(287.91)	0.00	(3.33)	8,349.09	1.91
Oakmark	45,265.00	0.00	357.25	0.00	0.79	45,622.25	10.44
PBHG Emerging Growth	28,403.00	0.00	1,141.02	0.00	4.02	29,544.02	6.76
Strong Small Cap	28,403.00	0.00	1,243.74	0.00	4.38	29,646.74	6.79
Third Avenue Small Cap	14,335.00	0.00	221.67	0.00	1.55	14,556.67	3.33
Warburg Pincus Emerging Markets	8,637.00	0.00	(343.23)	0.00	(3.97)	8,293.77	1.90
	427,158.00	0.00	3,190.27	0.00	0.75	430,348.27	98.52
CASH AND EQUIVALENTS		[Fees]					
Schwab Money Market Fund	6,472.05	0.00		0.00	0.00	6,472.05	1.48
	6,472.05	0.00		0.00	0.00	6,472.05	1.48
TOTAL PORTFOLIO	433,630.05	0.00	3,190.27	0.00	0.74	436,826.32	100.00

Figure 1.3 Performance by security, from an actual
client in 1997 for one week.

Whether it is about investments on Wall Street or individually owned annuities you have with insurance companies, people can relate to the constant bombardment of paperwork shuffled into your mailbox or inbox each month. The multiple-page reports include financial gibberish and lingo—not to mention a multitude of meaningless numbers—that would intimidate even the most seasoned investor. Many prospective clients, who frequently share with me these multiple-page reports, comment that they can't make heads or tails of them. Occasionally, I'll hear comments such as, "I don't open them anymore," or "All these statements do is create more worry, because I don't understand them anyway."

This all should make sense, as the game plan of the financial world to control consumer behavior heats up. The art of confusion to control and retain OPM is not limited to Wall Street and insurance companies; it applies to banks, the government— even the overconfident talking heads on radio and TV, whose livelihood, lest we forget, depends on you to listen to them and follow their opinions. My favorite talking heads are those who continually bash financial advisors like me, people who make their living from commissions or fees while at the same time neglecting to remind you that one of the purposes for their ramblings on TV and radio is to convince you to buy their books and materials, or whatever else they are peddling that day. What's the difference?

Our job in the financial world—including yours truly—is to convince you that we know what we're talking about so you will follow our advice and give us your money. We understand that working with your money (even if it is simply following advice from a book like this one) is part of the game. The hope is that it is a win-win for both of us. Regardless of whether the source is a financial advisor, attorney, certified public accountant (CPA), banker, insurance agent, investment advisor, or the talking head on radio or TV, we're all peddling something. That's our job; *your job* is to confirm that what we in the business are peddling is in *your* best interest—that the products and strategies are in line with who you are and what best suits your financial personality. *The 3 Personalities of Money* provides the confirmation you need to avoid the trappings of the one-size-fits-all mentality and all the differing views of peddling that are bombarding your mind on a daily basis.

CHAPTER 2

The Driving Force behind The 3 Personalities of Money

The 3 Personalities of Money gives you the ability to deal with all of the conflicting information and opinions out there about what you're supposed to do with your money.

We're going to delve into The 3 Personalities of Money shortly, but for now, here is a brief overview. The three are:

1. The Saver
2. The Investor
3. The Speculator

It's worth repeating that it is possible for one person to have personality traits of all three personalities. After visiting with thousands of consumers, I admit that few people are 100% of one financial personality. However, my research confirms that we all tend to have a predominant financial personality. The rest of this book will go into greater detail about these three personalities, but for now, let me give you brief definitions of each.

The Saver: First and foremost, savers are concerned with protecting what they've got—their principal. Although savers certainly want to earn as much interest as possible, they usually are not interested in putting their money at risk. They hate the idea of "losing" money. As the old saying goes, "They are more concerned with the return *of* their money than the return *on* it." Savers like to see and touch their money. This may explain why so many savers put money in the bank—they can drive by and/or walk in at any time, knowing the money is in the vault (actually, when you and I deposit money in the bank, very little of it ends up in the vault; instead, it is quickly loaned out to other people).

The Investor: This is the person who values the research and methodical process of thinking through investments before he or she makes a move. For instance, in the real world, an investor personality would never walk in to an appliance store to purchase a dishwasher without first researching a great deal about the various appliances and consulting objective consumer rating services. Investors do same thing with financial decisions and financial products. Investors will not take someone else's word for it, but want to confirm facts for themselves. Their hard-wiring gives them the confidence that, if given the right type of information, they can make up their own minds. That's why they are more likely than savers to take calculated risks with their money. Investors have a tendency to look long-term, thus being more comfortable with weathering some losses, as long as they are factored into the original decision.

The Speculator: Think of the happy-go-lucky guy in Vegas we talked about earlier. A speculator lives for the moment—for the thrill of trying to hit it big. It is all about the short term, the here and now. Money to the speculator is simply a tool to enjoy the moment. Money is merely a means to get there. Money, in and of itself, has little or no meaning, no attachment. It's simply a commodity to be used and enjoyed in the bigger game of life. A speculator believes that since money is round, it is meant to roll. Saving and investing money for the long term (buy, hold, and wait) is a foreign concept to most speculators.

Regardless of your predominant financial personality, some form of confusion or distress becomes the norm when you attempt to make financial choices. That's because of the barrage of one-size-fits-all messages. For instance, as of the date of this book, gold is being pushed as the last great stand before the dollar crashes into the abyss. You can't turn on the TV or radio without hearing about why you should be investing your life savings into the latest gold rush. Of course, we're all human, so who wants to miss out on this apparent safe haven? Never mind the fact that gold is, and has always been considered, a very speculative commodity—I'm constantly being asked by savers (people who in the past would never put their life savings into gold) if now is the time to load up on gold!

While we're on the subject of gold, allow me to share a funny story about gold and one's view on when to buy and when to sell. It also proves my point that someone can have traits of several financial personalities.

Over the past decades, I have hosted hundreds of financial workshops with thousands of people in attendance. I'm fortunate that I really get to walk in the financial shoes of so many different people from all backgrounds. This is one way I keep my pulse on what's going on in the world. Several years ago, an older gentleman in attendance at one of my workshops approached me as I was finishing up, and we had the following exchange:

"Hey, fella," the older gentleman said as he handed me a piece of paper, "You mind takin' a look at my stuff?"

"Sure, let me see what you got there," I respond. As I scan over the simple one-page handwritten document, I quickly notice a great deal of money in several different investments. "Wow, you've really done well for yourself, Sir! Notice a ton of Apple stock—how long have you had that?"

"Yeah, I've done alright," he says. "But now don't go messin' with my Apple stock, Sonny, I've had that a long time and ain't plannin' on sellin' all of it right now . . . been gradually takin' my winnins' off the table, though. What I want to know is what to do with all this money I got sittin' in the bank, earnin' squat?"

As I glanced down to the middle of the page, I noticed a specific line-item revealing several hundred thousand dollars in cash.

"Where did this money come from?" I ask.

"I sold all my gold," he proudly exclaimed.

"How come?" I ask.

Looking at me as if I have lost my mind, he says, "Cause, you nincompoop (that's what he called me), everybody's buyin' it!"

Moral to the story: The best time to sell, according to this very wealthy and wise older gentleman, is when everyone is buying. We can all learn a lot from this simple truth: Don't be a *nincompoop,* or in my words, "Don't follow the herd."

As long as we're on the subject of gold, here's another example of having one predominant financial personality and having a taste for another.

Let's say you just completed the 3 Personalities of Money test. You now have confirmed that—as in our example here—your predominant personality is investor. You weren't totally surprised by this, as you have always enjoyed researching the stock market and are comfortable with the ups and downs of it. Although you've made good money investing in blue-chip stocks (you love to buy and hold and those nice dividends that come with owning blue-chip stocks), you've noticed that option traders are making a ton of money betting on the direction of the price of gold, a highly speculative practice that is not for the faint of heart. You have studied these options for several years, but still feel they are very risky (this is your financial personality telling you to be careful). Nevertheless, you are starting to feel like you are really missing out on some big returns. So, with some hesitancy, you put 20% of your portfolio into the unfamiliar turf of trading options. In other words, you are predominantly still an investor, but could have a tendency to speculate if you feel that the return is worth it. Should the investor described in this example jump in? That's not for me to say without more information; I'm just pointing out how the mind works.

Let's take this example a little further. Let's assume a saver is standing at the water cooler, listening to this same investor confirm from another investor the potential benefits of gold options. The saver, who is fed up with 1% at the bank, doesn't want to miss out on this potential windfall of cash being discussed by these investors. Assuming these two investors know what they're talking about, the saver is convinced that gold is the place to be.

Fast-forward a few months later, when gold prices (and the saver's emotions) plunge downward. Our two investors, well aware that such a downturn could occur, accept the loss as part of the process of investing. They knew the gig before they took it. The poor saver panics, sells his position, takes a huge loss, and vows never to try that again!

One of the great investors of all time was Benjamin Graham (1894-1976). Mr. Graham, who is best known for his book *The Intelligent Investor*, was a major influence on one of today's most well-known investors, Warren Buffet. Graham, who was greatly concerned that savers and investors could unintentionally become speculators, had this to say, "An investment operation is one which, upon thorough analysis, promises safety of principal and a satisfactory return. Operations not meeting these requirements are speculative." Graham could see that people might end up in situations for which they weren't prepared.

Why try to pretend you're something you're not? To avoid trouble, just follow these three simple steps before investing:

First: Confirm your financial personality. Second: Learn to accept who you are and how you're wired—your financial personality. Third: Stop pretending you're something you are not, or investing in things you don't understand, or worse yet, things that aren't suited for you. Once you take these three steps, you will be more content with who you are and where to invest. You'll stop following the herd and begin focusing on financial products that are best for you; you'll toss aside those that aren't good for you. You'll save time instead of wasting it. Bottom line: You'll discover a worry-free world of simplicity and certainty as you stick to the things you know because of knowing who you are.

CHAPTER 3

Meet the 3 Personalities of Money

Personality 1: The Saver

Let's recall Benjamin Graham's definition of an investment in the previous chapter: "An investment operation is one which, upon thorough analysis, promises safety of principal and a satisfactory return. Operations not meeting these requirements are speculative."

If we apply Benjamin Graham's definition of "an investment operation" to the saver personality who bought into the notion of investing in a "portfolio" of diversified mutual funds (more than likely selected after taking a Risk Tolerance Questionnaire), must now consider themselves officially classified as new speculators!

Look at the definition again; a "true investment" assumes that you know what you are doing and that safety of principal plus a reasonable rate of return are at the core. Does that sound like you? Before you invest, do you really understand the risk involved? Are you taking all steps to avert a disaster? If the answer to these questions is, "Well, no, I'm not really doing that," then you are not a saver or an investor—you are officially a speculator.

If my granddad were still alive, as little as he knew about investing, he would agree 100% with Mr. Graham's statement. That's because true savers—like Granddad—admit they don't understand stocks and bonds enough to invest in them. A saver "knows" that he shouldn't take unnecessary risks with his money, and, if given the choice between 0% return or losing 20%, he will go with 0% every time. Problem is, much of the financial world isn't shooting straight with savers in terms of "real" risk—like the selections in the 401(k). Many of the mutual funds might look safe (review the definition again) but are they? Who knows!

The 3 Personalities of Money is long overdue. It simply states that some people have the financial genetics of savers, some of investors, and a small minority have the makeup of speculators. Nobody is 100% of just one financial personality, but everyone definitely has a predominant side. It really is that simple.

So why do many of today's consumers willingly follow the herd into areas of investing (or speculating) in products that go against their personalities—products that produce worry? The answer lies in the voices coming from the financial world—confident opinions leading consumers in all sorts of different directions. Granddad didn't hear such voices, because they weren't there. To my knowledge, he never discussed finances with any advisor. Today, confusing messages and mixed financial signals are everywhere.

Just this morning, as I was sipping my coffee and scanning the Wall Street Journal, *I found an article about a financial advisor whose main task in life is "continually convincing" his clients to hang in there with the stock market, even though it is apparent from this article that many of his clients are scared to death!*

Oh sure, if Granddad had wanted to, he could have taken the time and effort to run down to the local brokerage office, read the various stock quotes coming across the "wire" and talk to a stockbroker. Back then, stockbrokers actually did a lot of the research on individual stocks and bonds, rather than simply turning over your money to an outside money manager for a fee, as many of them do today.

So how did Wall Street (the voice of investors) find its way onto Main Street (the world of savers)? My theory: through the 401(k) plan.

Interestingly enough, most people in the 1940s were gun-shy of the stock market. In fact, according to Graham's book, The Intelligent Investor, *nearly 90% of them during that period of time wanted no part of the stock market, referring to it as gambling. These people had first-hand experience of the stock market crash just a few years earlier. Today, many unsuspecting savers have experienced the same type of losses due to stock market crashes of 2001 and 2008, thus suffering huge losses.*

Passed into law in 1978 (the same year my granddad retired), the 401(k) officially introduced Wall Street to Main Street. Up until this time, many workers were covered by their employer's pension plan. Like Granddad, the average worker didn't know anything about mutual funds, because he didn't need to know. His "savings plan" for retirement was being handled by his employer's pension plan. He had no need to pore over mutual fund selections, which was a good thing, since he and most of his hardworking working-class peers were savers. They appreciated the fact that their employer was safeguarding their money and their retirement. The days of the pension plan allowed workers to be worry-free. They weren't exposed to risk. In the pre-1978 days, the majority of employees were savers and knew it. They trusted their employer to provide their retirement income. Unfortunately, the introduction of the 401(k) plan allowed the representatives from Wall Street to show up at work and talk Joe Lunchbox into putting his life savings into the stock market, because that's what the 401(k) offered: mutual funds.

Following Graham's train of thought, this new investment approach of diversified portfolios of mutual funds for savers has ironically turned these unsuspecting folks into speculators! In fact, if I didn't know better, I'd say the lawmakers who came up with the idea of the 401(k) were in cahoots with Wall Street, as the lawmakers (and Uncle Sam) now sit on the sidelines, salivating for the huge amounts of tax revenue heading their way as 401(k) participants, many of whom have no idea how much in taxes they will owe one day, cash in these trillion-dollar government-sponsored slush funds, all adding up to one of the biggest deferred annuities for the government ever. The 401K certainly benefits Wall Street and Uncle Sam benefits Wall Street and Uncle Sam, while shifting all the risk and uncertainty to the saver.

By the way, prior to 2012, the custodians (big firms representing Wall Street) managing the mutual funds within your 401(k) were not required to disclose the fees charged by them to manage your funds. They do now, providing newfound proof of just how much Wall Street is making on your money. No wonder the financial world keeps telling us to put as much as we can into these 401(k) plans: You work hard, hand over your money to them, take all the risk, and leave the rest to them. Certainly, a profitable strategy of gaining other people's money for them, but I'm not so sure the consumer investing in the 401(k) is doing as well.

Without the 401K, there is no way that Wall Street could have gathered trillions (that's trillions with a "t") of dollars. The 401(k) paved the way for the Joe Lunchboxes (many savers who previously enjoyed guaranteed pension plans) to drift from the world of safety and security to the new world of risk and uncertainty. Savers don't understand the stock market and which mutual fund to select out of the "basket" of options with their 401(k) plan—and the financial world knows that. Yet, numerous financial institutions continue to successfully convince savers (sometimes through fear of running out of money) that the only way to be "worry-free" is to put your money at risk and "hang in there." Funny, my granddad never owned a stock or mutual fund, yet he was worry-free.

Are 401(k) plans a bad thing? Of course not; but contrary to popular belief, they are not the mother of all retirement plans either. In fact, many people I visit with are putting too much money into these plans. Why? Because they are following the herd of the one-size-fits-all 401(k) mantra of "max them out." There are so many considerations to be taken into account before ever contributing to a 401(k) plan. How much (if any) of the employee's contributions is the employer going to match? What tax bracket are you in today vs. where you might be in the future? How tax-diversified you are? What type of debt might you have that needs to be attacked before putting money into a 401k or other qualified plan such as this?

And while I agree that the 401(k) plan may be a convenient way to defer present tax liabilities, one must admit that there is control you give up, potential investment risk and the uncertainty of future taxes owed on the 401k money when you take it out. I call these "financial side-effects."

My beef is not whether 401(k) plans have merit, but whether millions of savers, investors, and speculators are fully aware of these considerations. After reading this section on 401(k) plans, you might want to sit down with a trained retirement specialist to confirm that maxing out is in your best interest. Slow down; step back and reevaluate the whole notion of the 401(k) and the selections, fees, and risk associated with them.

People come to me all the time wanting help with "which" mutual funds to choose within the many choices offered by the 401(k). I can't answer that question in this book; however, on a regular basis, I speak with federal government workers who are eligible for something referred to as a Thrift Savings Plan (TSP). Don't let the name fool you—it is just like a 401(k) plan. Basically, the Thrift is like a 401(k) plan in that it is a pretax means of stockpiling money for retirement. The difference is found in its simplicity of the investment options available. Within the Thrift is something called the G-Fund, or Government Securities Fund. For savers, this is the perfect fund! I just wish all 401(k) plans had this as well. So here's a worry-free hint: if you currently participate in a Thrift Plan and you have taken our free test to confirm that you are a saver, put your money in the G-Fund.

"But Tony," says the saver who has taken his or her eye off the ball and begun listening to the financial world's message to follow the herd into the stock market, "This isn't 1940 or 9/11. I'm sitting here making 2% in my "safe" investments while missing out on the latest 20% gains in the stock market. What am I supposed to do?"

Remember who you are, how you're wired, and your innate desire for safety, for guarantees. Keep your hand to the plow and don't look back. Learn as much as you can about all the safe investments out there (more on that in a minute) and learn how to minimize costs (much more on this in a minute). Make it your goal to be worry-free by avoiding things that keep you up at night. Commit to the things you know and believe in, and avoid the things you don't, knowing you're doing the best you can do with what you have. If you follow your heart and follow your personality, instead of following the herd, I guarantee you will be more content and worry less about your money.

The guiding principal of the saver is protection of principal. Don't forget that. A saver is hard-wired, born this way (nature) and/or he has personally experienced or witnessed someone else's experience or been taught (nurture) financial issues that relate to him. It is what it is. This simple truth of how savers respond to loss explains why so many Americans, limping out of the Depression, avoided the stock market in the 1940s. They experienced great loss or witnessed first-hand countless others lose it all, and they wanted no part of it. Those folks lived through it and knew the risk involved. They witnessed the devastation of losing it all and now they hate the thought of losing it again. These same people had children and, more than likely, taught them the same lessons of "play it safe and save as much as you can, because you never know what can happen."

Savers believe money is made by "working hard and saving hard." The thought of "losing" money relates back to the huge amount of time and effort it took to create their investments in the first place. Another reason a saver personality approaching retirement should never risk her money: savers don't have time to go back and repeat the whole process of working hard and saving hard. There is no time left for a do-over. Savers appreciate certainty and security and don't like surprises; uncertainty about the future is a major source of stress.

Some of the most disgruntled savers I meet are those who drank the financial Kool-Aid poured out by Wall Street during the go-go 1990s. They were convinced their hard-earned money was in conservative-growth mutual funds. The financial world and talking heads touted these so-called

conservative mutual funds as a can't-miss means of
securing a worry-free retirement.

Besides mutual funds being offered through the
401(k) plan, Joe Lunchbox was also introduced to
mutual funds through an unproven theory known
as "Buy term and invest the difference." This
concept reared its ugly head in the high-interest
environment of the 1980s, and was based on the
belief promoted by a former football coach, of all
folks, that nobody needed long-term whole-life
life insurance with its paltry 4% to 5% dividend
(which is what these contracts were paying, then as
well as now). Peddlers of this new train of thought
believed that one could make more money by
purchasing term life (short-term life insurance that
is much cheaper in premium—not necessarily in
cost—than whole life) and investing the difference
(the difference in the higher premium whole-life
vs. the lower premium term-life) in mutual funds.
At the time, with mutual funds making 12% to 15%
(much better than whole-life returns), why not! Fast
forward 30 years later, only to discover that Wall
Street representatives and talking heads on TV and
radio preaching this new, "one-size-fits-all" mantra
forgot to factor in the cost of the term life (a waste
of money, unless you die young), the fees charged
by the mutual funds—you had the commission
up front and the annual fees and finally, the huge
amount of taxes that can be generated by mutual
funds. Last but not least, worst part of all; nobody
made 12%! In fact, many of the "buy-term and

invest the difference" followers I have met have broke even or worse yet, have lost a bundle and have no life insurance to boot. Maybe this strategy would have worked for investors and speculators, but not for savers. That's because it goes against everything a saver believes: safety of principal and low cost. What's really comical is that just the other day, I heard one of these same talking heads who for years preached the wonders of easily making 12% in growth mutual funds now say that one should only assume about a 4% or 5% rate of return. While it's great that he's finally seen the light, that surely provides little comfort for all the people who for years followed his advice only to be led astray by it.

As someone who has studied the art of communications, let me tell you; there is a definite communication gap that exists between consumers and the financial experts regarding the lack of "concrete" words we can all agree on. *The 3 Personalities of Money* is dealing with this gap by focusing the conversation in ways never before done. For instance, when savers think of the word "conservative," they take it to mean "a plan in which money cannot be lost; it is conserved or protected." However, the word "conservative" to an investor from Wall Street might mean "less risk than other 'aggressive' investments." Much of the problem is the constant bombardment of ridiculous, vague concepts and terms that are deliberately left vague by the folks that create them. Wall Street gets to define the word "conservative" without really telling us what that means, for example.

The past few years have proved tragic in many ways. The events of 9/11, as well as the market crash of 2008, exposed savers to tragic losses. Many never recovered; they saw the market plunge and they bailed out. The people who suggested they invest in these obviously risky funds were the same people who told them to "Hang in there," another vague term requiring further explanation. Obviously, the definition of "conservative" and "hang in there" to the folks on Wall Street differed from the definitions held by savers. Of course, the 40-page, smaller-than-life printed prospectuses of these "conservative" mutual funds didn't help matters. Savers like simplicity, not 40-page legal documents. Most of them never read those documents.

This desire to avoid risk explains why most investors and speculators don't understand savers. Investors salivate over the prospects of reading and studying a 40-page document in hopes of growth; speculators, who aren't about to waste time and money on boring returns offered by "conservative" growth mutual funds, believe an aggressive plan of action is the only way to go. Savers trust in the certainty of things—the guarantee of a return of principal. Investors and speculators realize that change and uncertainty are part of the equation. Savers are oftentimes paranoid about others who offer to-good-to-be-true investments, particularly those that they perceive as unrealistic.

Now that we have defined the saver personality, it is worth noting that all is not lost when it comes to savers being able to use, enjoy, and grow their money. In fact, most of the savers who know who they are and what they can tolerate are the most contented people on Earth, especially when they are in the groove of working hard, keeping things simple, and saving money for the future in truly conservative financial products that they can easily and quickly quantify. Take a certificate of deposit (CD), a favorite tool of savers. It doesn't take a great deal of time and effort to calculate compound interest on a CD. It isn't that difficult to read a fixed-annuity statement either, or to understand the value of a government bond. That's what savers like—simple. That's not to say savers are not ambitious, but they aren't driven purely by the need to gain money at all costs either.

Another interesting characteristic of savers is their lack of interest in competing with the guy next door to see who can accumulate the most money and enjoy the biggest toys. One of my favorite books is *The Millionaire Next Door*. To me, this book, which seemingly consists of numerous interviews with what I refer to as savers, is basically about "folks next door" who happen to have boatloads of money; you just wouldn't know it by looking at them. The millionaire next door may drive a very modest car and live in a simple home.

These things represent the lives of savers. The millionaire next door reveals one of the best-kept secrets of savers: they really don't care what others think about what they've got.

To prove the point, I recently interviewed a couple in their mid-60s who admit to arguing only on one financial matter: the husband will not replace anything that he himself can fix. I asked for an example, to which his wife quickly chimed in (with a great deal of frustration in her voice) that their toaster is over 30 years old, yet she said, he *will not* replace it. His immediate response: "Why in the world would I spend money on a new toaster when the old one works just fine!"

Notice, he didn't frame it as a question but as a statement of fact; that's how savers view money and how to handle it. They will do what some might say is just, plain common sense.

Another "just plain common sense" notion that savers have is staying out of debt. My granddad always said, "If you can't afford it, don't buy it." Savers like Granddad didn't believe in debt. As far as I can tell, my granddad never borrowed money for anything. Sure, he had a small mortgage on his modest home in the country, but that was it. The closest thing to consumer debt for Granddad was a monthly charge account at the nearby general store. His total bill each month was 10 or 15 dollars, but he paid it off every month like clockwork. There was layaway in his day, but I don't think he ever participated in layaway. I guess he figured layaway still fit the mode of "If you can't pay cash for it now, don't lay it away."

With all this said, don't dismiss savers' ability to manage businesses. Many have proved to be very good business people. That's because savers are so good at holding on to money. They understand the value of a dollar and realize that keeping costs in check is the key to profitability and growth; out-of-control costs may be the major reason for businesses' failure. A saver has the work ethic and fortitude to put off today what will reap benefits in the future. Unlike a speculator, who doesn't have the patience to wait around for something to materialize in 20 years, the saver is comfortable with a slow-and-steady, long-term approach. Savers are patient and know that what a man sows, so shall he one day reap. As we've mentioned earlier, savers value hard work and believe that things just don't happen overnight. They feel you should get an honest wage for an honest day's work. I think that's why so many savers have distaste for the stock market and the folks at Wall Street pushing their products. They see Wall Street types in three-piece suits making multimillion-dollar bonuses, and for what?

If much of what I'm describing sounds like you, you're probably a saver. To confirm it, simply go to our free testing site at 3Personalities.com.

Personality 2: The Investor

Savers make up the majority of the population, and investors are definitely the second most prevalent financial personality. Unlike savers, investors are not as concerned with protection of principal. While it is true investors have no intention of losing money, they do understand the inherent risks associated with investments and the strategies that fit their personality. They understand that it takes money to make money—that investments can fail and principal will fluctuate. My late father-in-law was definitely an investor. He had several stocks that went down in flames in 2008; however, his comment to me was that he still knew they were good dividend-paying companies, and he would ride it out. As he predicted, the stocks did come back and all was well again in Mudville.

An investor relishes the prospects of taking calculated risks with money—money she wishes to grow above the normal interest rates typically enjoyed by the saver. Investors know there are different financial tools and products for different situations, and they accept the challenge of finding them. And that's not just researching financial products; it includes anything that has to do with investing and spending money.

For instance, let's say an investor is in the market for a new dishwasher. What's the first thing she will do? Run over to the first appliance store, talk to a salesman for two minutes and make the purchase? Of course not! The saver or speculator may operate this way, but not the investor. The investor personality must discover and confirm what is the best buy before plunking down the money. The investor knows there are other experts who have done their homework, even when it comes to dishwashers. The investor isn't simply going to take the dishwasher salesman's word as to the best model. No, the investor is going to find that out herself. Her analytical skills and search for the best buy will take over. Time spent on this matter is of no issue. In fact, the time spent on this search for the best buy is time well-spent. Otherwise, if the investor doesn't go this routine of research, she will forever question herself as to whether everything was done to confirm that she in fact did get the best buy.

Investing money is no different. Investors don't just stop in the local bank and stash money in a bank CD. Instead, they will tend to research all the options for investing, even if it is a very conservative investment like a CD. Again, investors want to feel like they are ahead of the curve. They feel they are smart enough to do so when it comes to buying decisions and investing. The investor's definition of "conservative" says that he needs to invest in things that will at least beat the rate of inflation, and he will take the time to look and find it. In other words, the investor won't feel good about having the highest CD rate in town, having the highest government bond yield, or having all of his money in a fixed annuity, because he knows these products will more than likely struggle to keep up with inflation. And while savers tend to be more trusting of others (the nice young man selling dishwashers or the nice young man down the hall at the local bank will more easily gain the trust of the saver than he will of the investor), investors have a skeptical streak. They are not as easily influenced by others or by outside forces, but would rather put their faith and trust in their own abilities to discover for themselves what's best. Their personality is marked by a quiet confidence in researching and processing different information in order to come to a logical conclusion.

They will be comfortable with risk when they have researched all options. Investors don't fear the stock market, as most savers do. They analyze it and seek to understand it, and they enjoy the process. They look at things logically, and their decisions aren't generally swayed by their emotions. This tendency toward research doesn't just apply to the stock market; these personalities do their homework before buying an appliance or choosing a doctor or making any other significant decision.

Investors aren't impulsive. However, they value flexibility, so they can make changes when their research convinces them they should. Control is important, because they never stop looking for a better way. And as results improve, expectations rise.

Validation is important to investors. They view history as a source of reassurance, yet they stay on top of what's current, because they recognize that things change. True validation only comes through independent research. Risk is not something to be avoided. What matters is that the risks are known and that they are outweighed by potential benefits. Investors are patient and are not easily excited. The excitement kicks in when new information contradicts their conclusions and it's time to reevaluate. When the market crashed in 2008, investors saw the downturn as an opportunity, not as a loss. They are only likely to become upset if they overlooked details or missed something that made their methods unreliable.

Personality 3: The Speculator

True speculators are rare. In fact, when contacting random subjects to complete our testing for the 3 Personalities of Money Financial Profile, we struggled to find speculators. Prior to our research, I had always assumed that speculators made up approximately 2% of the general population, but as I weigh the subject more, I'd say the percent of speculators is less than 1/10 of 1%, or .001. That hasn't been confirmed, simply observed. Speculators can perhaps best be described as the daredevils of the financial world. Like any daredevils, speculators are thrill-seekers and relish the thought of hitting it big. Risk is not a deterrent and patience is not one of their virtues.

They love competition, sometimes to the point of being aggressive. They thrive on challenges. They may desire domination of the situation at hand—financially, personally, professionally, in every respect. Just tune in to one of those poker games and watch the participants very closely. This is all about beating your competitor for money. It is about winning. The very thought of a saver like Granddad sitting at a poker table, donning dark sun glasses and a baseball cap, staring stone-faced at the other poker players is a comical visual indeed. Another aspect of speculators is their outspoken personality. They love to tell and show how well they're doing. The high roller that pulls up in the big car with loads of cash is a good visual. Donald Trump comes to mind as someone who enjoys the limelight and likes reminding everyone about his billions. Speculators can be very funny and the life of the party. Most speculators are actually quite generous with their money, which makes sense when you think about it, as their motto of "Easy come, easy go" fits right into the idea of living for today and not worrying about tomorrow. They are typically outspoken, enthusiastic, expressive, upbeat, compulsive, impulsive, resistant to cautions or criticism, and sometimes volatile.

These personalities trust their gut. They chase the emotional highs they get from the gamble with confidence that things will turn out in their favor, at least in the long run. Speculators are willing to take advantage of situations, and even people, and they view loss as an inevitable part of the game.

They often view personal relationships as part of the game, too, making them hard to maintain. Speculators are usually exceptionally friendly, life-of-the-party types, but relationships remain superficial and may be sacrificed if someone is seen to be holding the speculator back.

Speculators can be overconfident, dismissive of their own difficulties, and unfazed by failure. In many cases, they are not sensitive to the plight of others or to how their own behavior can affect others, sometimes in negative ways. Their competitive nature takes the attitude, "Tough luck for losers." And speculators don't understand the other personalities; needs like security and traits like patience are foreign and incomprehensible.

Their driving characteristics can get speculators into trouble, especially when they see someone else getting what they want. For example, if a speculator watches someone clean up in a few hands of poker, he's likely to jump into the game, assuming he can do the same, but better.

Speculators view money as a means to an end. It is a tool for enjoying life, for gambling with, and for dominating. There's an easy come, easy go attitude, with the belief that lost money can simply be made up next time. They want control over their money, and more specifically, access to it at all times to suit their whims.

If this description seems to characterize you, you are probably one of that rare and fascinating breed I call a speculator.

A word of caution to speculators (please don't take this personally, as I know you won't anyway): you truly are a rare breed. I'm not assuming you should try to change; just keep in mind that this mindset of always hitting it big can get you and others in deep trouble. In fact, I've seen this play out with one of my clients who, I later discovered, had a gambling addiction. It got so bad that he began taking lines of credit from his credit cards and going back to the poker table to try to make up for his losses. It got so bad that he finally lost it all. I asked him why he kept gambling and his response was that he thought he really could win it all back. Luckily, he still has his wife and kids, but that's about it.

My brother, who is a drug and alcohol counselor, says that the most difficult addiction to break is gambling. According to him, like alcohol and drugs, you have the addiction component you're trying to break (which is hard enough as it is), but with gambling, you also have this additional component of competition and drive that feeds another emotional high, which is very addictive as well. So with that warning, if you are a speculator, be careful.

Does the name *Demetrios Georgios Synodinos* ring a bell? No? How about his other name, Jimmy "the Greek" Snyder? Thought that might ring a bell. Best known for his colorful sports commentary on *The NFL Today* show, "Jimmy the Greek" started his speculative career in the oil and gas business. Jimmy definitely was comfortable with his financial personality. After flunking out of the oil and gas business, Jimmy took his speculative personality to Las Vegas where, in 1956, he began focusing on sports—specifically, of all things, pro football betting. His experience in the field of pro football led to a 12-year stint on the CBS Sunday morning football show, *The NFL Today*. He was fired by CBS Sports in 1988 after a controversial comment about race.

Jimmy the Greek was definitely entertaining. His usual deal was to appear at halftime of NFL football games, giving his take on things and sending signals as to what would be your best bet about the game. Speculators loved to hear Jimmy go on about the odds, the what-ifs, the variables, the major factors, and why they should bet on one outcome or another. And while I remember my dad (who was a saver) enjoyed Jimmy's comments, he never had clue as to what Jimmy was talking about or why anyone would be gambling their hard-earned money on football games. Jimmy the Greek had his facts and data and tidy presentations, but most people knew in the end it was mostly posturing based on hopes and hunches and that, ultimately, luck played as much a role—or more of one—as anything else.

Yet, that's okay for speculators (which Jimmy the Greek certainly was). It's all part of the fun. You want to hit it big, and preferably quickly. Making investments or gambles with your money is just a means to that end.

However, if you are a speculator, you've come to realize that most people in the financial world do not understand your financial personality. Some might even think you are nuts! But in your competitive and confident mind, you feel that your desire to invest in speculative high-risk endeavors offering potentially very high returns is no different from Wall Street, for instance, taking savers' money and blindly throwing it in some stock. Either way, you figure (and in my opinion, rightly so) everyone is after the same thing; trying to make as much money as they can. Your rub with the financial world is the fact that you know better and sure don't want to hand your money over to someone else to use and control. They keep promising you a slow and steady long-term growth rate on your money, while you respond, "So what!" They'll tell you to keep some of your money in a safe place and you say, "Why?" Yawn . . . What good is your money if it's out of your hands? What is there to like about "slowly but surely?" What's fun about staying safe?

As we look over what's been said about all three types of financial personalities, one piece of advice is common to all three. Don't neglect your financial personality—you are uniquely hard-wired a certain way and that's that.

The financial world doesn't know what your money personality is, so how can anyone in it possibly provide you with advice that speaks to who you are? How can they be expected to guide you toward what you need and want? If they don't know what you're looking for, they're in no position to help you find it.

They're just doing their jobs. It's up to you to look out for number one. You're responsible for yourself and your own happiness or lack thereof. You've shown initiative by picking up this book.

You've demonstrated an interest in figuring out what's going on with you and your money. And, since you're still reading, the 3 Personalities of Money concept is obviously speaking to you in a relevant way.

And, if you'll let me toot my own horn, I'm not surprised; it all makes sense. I've seen the money personalities emerge time and time again in the course of my own financial practice, in talking to friends, clients and associates, and numerous interviews with consumers and financial experts. The concept is sound.

I've also seen the results of ignoring the money personalities time and time again. I've seen the stress, the anxiety, the sleepless nights, and the financial paralysis. I've seen how people are troubled by self-serving advice from the financial world. I've seen a lot of struggle and insecurity. But it doesn't have to be that way.

You've taken the first step to change things. Now it's up to you to be proactive. Start by resolving to learn more about your financial personality. If you have not done so, take three minutes to take the free personality test by logging on to 3Personalities.com. Don't neglect your financial personality.

Maybe you're saying, "OK, Tony, I get it. I recognized a lot of myself in one of the 3 Personalities of Money being discussed in this book. I took the free test. Now I know what my financial personality is. I'm with you . . . now what? How do I put this newfound knowledge to work for me?"

Don't worry. I didn't write this book to waste your time. I would never pose a problem without providing a solution. The rest of this book is all about how you're supposed to use this information. Read on.

CHAPTER 4

Honoring Your Financial Personality

*Define what you don't know as well as
what you do know and stick to what you
know.*
                    —*Warren Buffett*

If you don't know what you're looking for, it's
pretty hard to find it. However, once you know who
you are, you can begin to stick to what you know,
thus "finding" whatever it is in life you are looking
for. Sounds confusing, but it's really very simple.

Defining your financial personality is crucial to
understanding what you're looking for and how to
best go about finding it. Maybe you need security
and certainty, maybe you want the opportunity to
learn and plan and grow, or maybe you're after
thrills on the hunt for the big payoff.

The financial world doesn't make it easy to figure this stuff out. Its game plan is one of confusion—to keep you thinking you need them. Sometimes, its game plan includes promoting fear of loss if you don't follow their lead or, worse yet, giving you the idea that without them you'll end up in the poorhouse. Unrealistic projections of what you'll need one day for retirement provide even more worry for consumers. Their "general rule of thumb" says that in order to enjoy a worry-free retirement, one must have saved enough money to generate 80% of your pre-retirement income. Sadly, this is simply a case of shooting from the hip! No wonder consumers are staying up at night, wondering how they'll ever make it . . . very few people I encounter have enough money to replace 80% of their working income. I see a lot of people, and most of the hard-working average folks I work with do not have this much money. The truth is, the one-size-fits-all claim of the financial world make it on much less than you think.

One of my favorite "unrealistic" views of "what we need" is the well-played commercial on television showing people walking around carrying large pieces of cardboard with numbers on them. One person's savings needed (before he can apparently retire in comfort) is $1,800,000; another person's cardboard cutout reads $2,340,000 . . . to which the announcer chimes in, "Let us help you with your magic number!" To which I reply, "You've got to be kidding me!"

Not only is this ad inaccurate, but worse yet, it leaves the vast majority of viewers with a gut-wrenching feeling of discouragement as they ponder the fact that their number is nowhere near the magic number selected by the financial world. Never fear, because your number is *your* number . . . not theirs! Do not allow the financial world to put on you the guilt-trip gospel of not having enough according to their standards and their prospective pocketbooks. Remember the message of confusion and keeping you in fear of your future; if they can pull that off, they figure you'll gladly hand over your money to them.

Folks, we don't need more goofy ads from the financial world. What we need—and what you now have—is a means of discovering what will allow you to be worry free. *The 3 Personalities of Money* guards your heart and mind from all the noise and arbitrary notions of money. It takes the approach that money is simply a commodity to be used, saved, invested, and enjoyed differently by different people. It is based on science and common sense, not some "magic number" pulled from thin air by others who know nothing about you. While we certainly need and appreciate the financial world's products, we don't have to allow them to dictate the terms of our financial happiness.

Several years ago, I was asked to speak to some 300 advisors who specialize in working with savers—my peers—at a conference (in Vegas of all places) about my philosophy of money so I could tell more about my story and why so many consumers appear attracted to it. Much to their surprise, instead of telling my story, I told them the story of my granddad (a true saver), someone whom I admired a great deal. As I stated earlier, when it came to money, as far as I could tell, Granddad never had a "financial planner" or "financial advisor." Heck, he could have cared less about some number that he was supposed to have stockpiled for retirement. What he did know was that if he worked hard, spent money only if he really had it, and kept his nose clean, one day, he and his faithful wife Hazel would receive what his employer had always promised, something Granddad referred to as "mailbox money".

In other words, Granddad worked all those years with the phone company until he retired in 1978 and received his pension. To my knowledge, he never knew the rate of return on the pension plan, but he sure got his money back, guaranteed for the rest of his and Hazel's lifetime. I've attached the original letter Granddad received from his employer's pension. Not a lot of money, you say? Well, all I can tell you is that my beloved granddad, living on his whopping pension of less than $1,000 a month and his monthly Social Security of not much more, was truly worry free.

Now before you think I've gone off the deep end, let's be quite clear: I'm not saying you should take the approach of Granddad and live a life of frugality. I'm not at all implying that you should not secure/hire the services of a financial advisor (of which I am one). I'm not saying to tune out the experts who are open about what they know and what they don't. I'm not saying to never consult an expert; sometimes you have to. What I am saying is that understanding your financial personality (as my granddad instinctively knew) is THE most important step—the first step you should take—to simplifying your life and getting your finances in order with the least amount of worry and stress. Operating in accordance with the way you're wired to think about money is the key to dealing successfully with savings and investments.

Other people from the financial world are simply there to provide additional tools and resources to guide you along the way to a worry-free retirement. People like me are here to honestly point out things you may not be aware of, to use our experience to see things that the average consumer may not be aware of, and to keep you out of trouble. The rest is up to you, as it should be.

But don't count on everyone in the financial world to put their interests aside in exchange for the benefit of yours. Don't think they'll always guide you to lifelong security or happiness or Shambhala. Keep in mind how the game is played: The more fear and uncertainty they can instill in us, the more likely we are to put our money with them. Remember, that's how they make their living, from other people's money (OPM). None of us in the financial world are financial saints or prophets. We have our financial warts, just like you. We are human, and as much as we try to remain objective, we too, have experiences that can cloud our thinking and our advice. We can be tempted to say and do things we shouldn't. That's why you'd better know who you are and be confident of what is best for you. Think of it as the moat around your financial castle.

Even as I write this, it reminds me of why I am so passionate about this new line of thinking: this mind-over-money concept that works so well and makes so much more sense than the one-size-fits-all mentality.

CHAPTER 5

When Savers Become Investors

"But Tony," you ask. "Isn't the field of behavioral finance dealing with this very issue of psychology and money?"

In my view, the growing trend to bring behavioral finance into the mix is missing the mark. That's because, once again, behavioral finance is trying to make sense of "why" people make financial decisions (often with the assumption that consumers are wrong in their timing of the market, that they don't "hang in there" long enough, and other such irrelevant concepts regarding people and money). Behavioral finance relies on the theory that we all act on emotions rather than logic and facts. The behavioral finance world—at least when it is utilized by the financial world—assumes that consumer emotions are irrational because someone reacts differently than others to the same circumstances—one person sells when the market drops, the other hangs in there with the belief that the market will come back. *The 3 Personalities of Money* says stick with who you are and what you know; first consider how much money needs to be in the stock market, if any at all. This way, the emotional roller coaster is taken out of the equation.

Evidence provided by various independent research firms has proven that over the past 20 years (for example), the average "diversified" investor portfolio performed poorly compared to the return of the Standard and Poor's (S & P) 500 index. Baffled as to why most investors fall behind, these same "independent" research folks attribute such shabby results to poor market timing, irrational decisions and/or other emotional issues affecting their decisions. Of course, one of my favorite level-headed investors, the founder of Vanguard, John Bogle, has always contended, that over the long term, most people cannot beat the market, especially when you add in all the fees that portfolio managers charge for trying to do so. If you're interested in finding out more about this, I suggest you read his book, *John Bogle on Investing: The First 50 Years.* It is a real eye-opener and will help explain much of what continues to dismay the so-called independent experts.

In my view, the problem of the average investor performing so poorly, even though he followed the herd to "diversification," is not found in people's emotions, but the fact that most of these people are savers, not investors. In other words, if you could test these so-called investors to see if they are in fact investors, you would find that most of them are really savers. Which means savers are investing in things they should not be investing in. That's the problem! In short, the samplings used in these studies are skewed with too many people in the sample that don't belong there in the first place. In other words, get the savers out of the market; then see what the "average" investor earns, and my guess is that it would be much higher.

If you're an investor, be careful not to allow studies such as the independent research studies mentioned above to sway you. My guess is that after reading them, some investors may grow needlessly worried, questioning themselves because others are doing so poorly, when in reality, a true investor may have done better than the normal benchmarks currently used, i.e., the S&P 500. If you are an investor, by all means utilize the expertise of others in the field who you feel are qualified to help you; just don't forget that you also bring a great deal of research skills and knowledge to the table.

Although there's nothing wrong with throwing your emotions into the mix, it is much more important to never forget who you are and what you are most comfortable with. Know and follow your true financial personality.

CHAPTER 6

Applying the 3 Personalities of Money:

Basic Approaches to Personality-Based
Money Management

You've met the 3 Personalities of Money. You got to know them a little and you've identified closely with one. Hopefully by now, you've taken the 3-minute test and know which personality reflects your instincts, attitudes, fears, goals, and ultimately, who you are when you think about and deal with money. Hopefully, you've learned something about yourself.

I've learned some things about you, too. This information is important. It's exactly what's missing whenever voices from the financial world try to speak to you in a relevant way.

Now, I'd like to show you how to apply this newfound knowledge toward making your life simpler and more worry free. I'm dedicating the second section of this book to illustrating how the 3 Personalities of Money concept can revolutionize the way you approach your savings and investments.

What you've been reading isn't some theoretical self-help psychobabble. It has real-world implications and applications. Once you start looking at your finances through the lens of your money personality, the right course of action in any financial situation becomes a lot clearer. As you get the hang of it, you'll function as your own financial advisor. And you'll be better at it than anyone else. Read on to see exactly what I mean about practical applications. Remember, when it comes to money management, as I've stressed throughout this book, one size does not fit all. The basic strategy you adopt sets the stage for how stressful or worry-free your financial life will be.

I don't mean to imply that every saver, every investor, and every speculator should do exactly the same things with their money as their personality counterparts. As I've said, everybody can have a little of the other personalities in them to varying degrees, and everyone's needs and wants are unique. But you can benefit greatly from starting out with an attitude and an approach that suits who you are at a fundamental level.

I'll start by offering some basic guidelines about how each money personality should approach savings, investments, and general financial planning. Take the advice to heart and let it inform your initial money management decisions.

The Saver

You've seen what happens when money runs out. You know what struggle is. You know what it means to climb your way out of a hole that has swallowed you. You've been through it, or maybe your parents or someone else close to you went through it. Perhaps your parents lived through the Great Depression, and lived a frugal, cautious life, having seen how desperate things can get.

Regardless of the details behind the scenes of who you are as a saver, protecting your money is your financial priority. This makes you wary of the stock market and risk in general. You also don't have the inclination to spend hours researching and learning about stocks, bonds, mutual funds, real estate prospects, or other investments. Frankly, you'd rather spend that time with your family or on a hobby.

With your money personality in mind, it's an easy call to recommend that you keep things relatively safe and simple. A savings account is your safety net, providing the peace of mind that comes with unrestricted access to your money in case of an emergency. You probably already have a regular schedule of deposits.

But don't stop at a savings account. There are a number of other conservative options. Save the majority of your money in financial products like bank certificates of deposit (CDs), traditional and fixed indexed annuities, permanent life insurance, particularly dividend-paying whole life insurance (DPWL), government treasury bills (T-bills), and/or government or high-grade corporate bonds and/or bond exchange-traded funds (ETFs). And maybe you'll decide to put a little money into the stock market. If so, you more than likely will want to stick to solid blue-chip stocks (the IBMs of the world) that pay consistent dividends.

As a saver, you are not fond of paying fees and penalties for managing or accessing your money. Fees on your money will have a dramatic effect on your net worth and will create many sleepless nights. When you discover the potential fees charged by Wall Street, well, to say you'll need to change the batteries in your financial pacemaker would be an understatement. As you can see, with fees, the financial world can make more money on your money than you do. That doesn't sit well with savers.

In addition to guarantees and avoiding fees, as a saver, you appreciate accessibility, simplicity, and avoiding other costs such as interest on loans, taxes, and unnecessary insurance premiums. One point: even though the fees charged by Wall Street may seem high, if you'd like to mix in some solid blue-chip stocks and good-quality bonds, you still may be served by a stockbroker who can help you select them. If you are leaning toward mutual funds, try to find an advisor or brokerage company, such as Vanguard, who will select very low-cost, low-turnover mutual funds (which means you'll pay lower taxes) containing characteristics suited to your conservative nature. When approaching something new, find out about the potential charges you may incur down the road. This goes a long way toward preventing aggravation. Also, be on the lookout for taxes created by bonds and certificates of deposit. That's because the more interest you make, the more (the government) takes. If you're finding that interest is getting taxed too heavily, consider having the dividends and interest paid to you in cash rather than reinvesting it. That'll at least flatten the tax.

Give your time to your family and friends, your hobbies and passions, the work you enjoy, and whatever else makes you happy. Don't get caught up in the manufactured worry about whether you're doing enough with your money. In the long run, the stress of fighting against your money personality takes more of a toll than it's worth. You save diligently toward goals; don't hesitate to spend some money where you intended it to go. When you work hard toward something, you've earned it.

The Investor

By nature, you research, analyze, study, and inform
yourself. So get to it. There's a whole world of
options out there, and you'll be happiest if you
set out to discover and understand them. There's
a whole spectrum of risk, too, and you'll want to
know all about it, as well.

Approach money management as you would go
about buying an expensive new appliance. A lot of
people run out to their favorite store, maybe ask the
friendly sales associate a few quick questions, and
buy the model with the most familiar name. But not
you! Before you drop big bucks on anything, you
do your homework, because you see the appliance
as an investment. All the brands—big and small—
are in the running. You visit different stores and
websites to examine selections and compare prices.
You read expert and consumer reviews. And during
it all, you enjoy yourself. Regarding fees charged
for services to manage your money, you may
be better served in going with a low-cost online
brokerage service. Do this, of course, only if you're
comfortable in going it alone.

This same effort should go into the decisions
you make for your money whenever you get
involved in anything where value can decrease.
Only by devoting this level of time and attention
will you truly be comfortable with investments.
You have to know how each investment works
and what sort of track record it has. You need to

understand the risks involved and to perform your own risk-benefit analysis.

But be wary of getting bogged down in the investigation and becoming paralyzed. There's always the concern that you haven't done enough research, that you've overlooked some detail, and that you haven't looked well enough to leap yet. Have some faith and don't second-guess yourself. When you've reached a decision, go with it. Remember, while you can minimize risks, there are never guarantees in life, no matter how much homework you do.

As an investor, you'll definitely want some of your money kept safe. You may appreciate that real gains only come with risk, but you're not looking to lay it all on the line and go for broke. Put some of your funds in conservative picks like bank certificates of deposit (CDs), fixed annuities, and government bonds, or high-grade corporate bonds, and/or bond exchange-traded funds (ETFs).

Just don't put too much away in the safe stuff. You'll be dissatisfied with low interest rates and the sense that your money isn't growing. And you'll get bored. Seek out options that reward your diligence and your smarts. You should enjoy getting into the stock market and real estate. Some investors go for riskier opportunities, too. Feel out your comfort level as you go.

The Speculator

You're more of a gambler than an investor. You do invest your money, but it's for the thrill of chasing the big score. Long-term thinking means short-term lost opportunity costs. You admittedly lack the patience to sit around and wait for bonds to mature or to be overexcited with 4% stock dividends and fixed annuities. To you, slow and steady is too boring. You're looking to win, pure and simple, and the prospect of losing doesn't deter you. Money is simply a commodity for playing the game.

You're a rare breed. As mentioned earlier, after decades of finance experience, I'll venture that you are in the "less than 1%" (where have I heard that before?) of the population that is wired for speculation.

"Risk!" you say. To you, that's half the fun of the game. Without risk (and lots of it) there is NO true reward. You define reward as "bountiful" return. None of this paltry talk of 6% to 7% . . . we're talking 15% to 20% to 100%! The reason I know this is because I have met some of you who have routinely made this much money in various ventures. Obviously, just like fishing, there are always those big ones that just got away, but hey, that's part of the adventure. You probably know that people will feel awkward around your financial endeavors. They may not even understand you—especially your good friends and family members. Don't fight the feeling . . . just keep it

in check and be sure to keep something back, just
in case. And please, if you have family who are
dependent on you, at least get some life insurance
on yourself in case the dreams don't plan out. A
large life insurance policy on yourself, payable
to your family, will make both you and them feel
much more secure. That's because—and I know
you'll appreciate these odds—there is a 100%
chance of you dying one day. That's something I
can guarantee.

Put your money where your mouth—or
your gut—is. That's how your personality finds
satisfaction. You're smart, and you have instincts
for how to win out in the long run. You have the
stomach to ride things out long after most others
have jumped ship, and that's a big part of how
you succeed. Even if you can't be bothered with
the details, and even when it doesn't look like it
to those around you, you understand what you're
doing.

You'll always regret the money that's sitting
out on the sidelines. Don't leave more than you
need to in savings or in wimpy investments. For
you, there's too much opportunity out there in
riskier propositions. Futures, options, initial public
offerings of stocks (IPOs), commodities, and other
high-risk routes are your territory.

You'll need to ignore a lot of what the financial
world says. Their constant mantra promoting
various financial products usually isn't meant for
you. Maxing out your 401(k) is not going to send

chills up your financial spine. That's because the investments within the plan aren't tempting or extremely rewarding. Don't feel guilty. Most people around you don't see things as you do and aren't likely to understand or approve of your decisions; take care not to alienate them. Try to compromise with your spouse. Keep your loved one in the loop and let him or her be involved in the finances. Never put all your eggs in one basket. Make sure some money is tucked away safely, too; it brings peace of mind for your family; it's there in case things go badly, and some should be set aside in case some new investment opportunity comes along.

For those of you reading this section that live with a speculator, but cannot understand the person's financial hard-wiring, just think of the miner 49ers of the California gold rush in the 1800s. Thousands of these faithful souls truly believed they could leave everything behind and come back millionaires. (The call was: "There's gold in them-there hills!") Those fellows were true speculators. They left their homes, risking everything for the allure of hitting it big. They speculated that with some hard work and a lot of luck, they would strike gold and make it big. The speculation of it all was the fact that there was no way in heck a man could be assured of finding gold. It's the same today . . . you can invest in gold because you think the dollar will fall and everyone will want your gold, but that is speculation. There is really no basis to your thinking—just as easily as gold can continue to climb in value, its value could plummet. As we speak, the same thing is happening with home values. People are purchasing homes that are under water in hopes of "flipping" them (reselling them in a short time for a higher value) and making a bunch of money. That may pan out; on the other hand, it could be that the reason you got such a good buy is that you are the only one that is currently willing to pay the price you just paid. That would be called speculation.

CHAPTER 7

Common Investment Questions and the Best Answers for You

Now that I've covered some general approaches to money management for each of the 3 Personalities of Money, let's get more specific. I assured you this concept would let you serve as your own financial advisor. And I meant it. To prove it, I'm going to address some of the most common questions people have when they consult a financial advisor.

I'll pose a question, and then I'll answer it for each personality type. This will illustrate how you can approach financial decisions, while considering your money personality. You'll see questions with fresh eyes and learn a new way to mull over the possible answers. Ready?

Should I take part in my company's 401(k) plan?

Savers: A 401(k) is appealing as a convenient way to save toward retirement. Although mutual funds may appear safe, your money is generally at risk there. Still, you'll be enticed by your employer's matching (up to a certain percentage) the amount of your paycheck that you put away, Suggestion: Contribute enough money to the 401k in order to take advantage of your employer's match. If your employer doesn't match your contributions, consider other alternatives that might provide more flexibility in your overall planning. Other options might include a Roth IRA, bank insured products, and even permanent life insurance, just to name a few.

Investors: A 401(k) may work for you if you contribute up to the point your employer matches your contributions. You'll always be aware that your money is at risk in mutual funds in a manner that's out of your control, though, and it will feel somewhat like speculating to you. You also might be frustrated by the unimpressive growth. Don't rule out contributing up to the point of the employer match, but also look into starting an IRA or putting your money into more promising individual investments with better tax treatment, lower fees, and more flexibility.

Speculators: A 401(k) means you don't know what the institution holding your money is charging you, you have no control over what they're investing your money in, there are very limited investment opportunities, and there are strict limitations on accessing your money without getting taxed to death, you need a permission slip from the government just to touch your money, and there's no shot at a big score. Sound good? Didn't think so. Unless you really need a place to safely store some money toward retirement, maybe for your spouse's peace of mind, take your money and run!

Where should I invest the money I've already put into a 401(k) or other government-sponsored plan?

Savers: You're on the government's terms as to what you can do with this money. Keep in mind that the vast majority of funds within your plan are risky. Check whether your plan offers some sort of government-backed securities fund. If it doesn't, look for a stable value fund or corporate bond fund. Put at least 60% to 80% of the 401(k)-invested money into these funds. This largely keeps you off the roller coaster ride of the stock market so you can sleep at night. You're looking primarily for safety, not growth.

If there are no safe options and you can't pull your money out, don't contribute more money into the plan unless your employer is matching. Don't put in a penny more than is matched. Otherwise, you'd be better off opening a traditional IRA or a Roth IRA and putting new money in the bank or in an insurance company with fixed annuities or life insurance, or in a government-backed instrument. Remember, free money from your employer may sound great, but what good is it if it's lost?

Investors: You don't appreciate losing control over your money and the difficulty of planning for the eventual tax liability. You'll feel better selecting your own investments and planning the tax bill yourself. If you feel good about the company you work for, find out if you can get stock as part of the 401(k) plan. Don't get hung up on past performance of funds in your plan; it doesn't mean anything. Decide which funds look good for the future. For example, if technology seems promising, opt for funds leaning toward tech stocks. Don't fall for the "diversification" line, buying a little of everything. If you're going to diversify your growth away, just play it safe and put your money in government-backed securities or stable-value funds.

One other thought: if you feel like you have too much money in your 401(k), don't panic, you may have some recourse. Contact the plan administrator to see if you are eligible for something referred to as "non-hardship, in-service withdrawal." This provision allows employees over the age of 59 ½ to roll out 401k funds to their own individual IRA. My advice, if you can roll out money without penalty, go ahead and do it.

Speculators: The 401(k) and other government-sponsored plans are not for you. There's far too little control and you definitely don't like the government setting the rules. If you have old money floating around in a plan, look into getting it out of there. If it's stuck, figure out which funds best suit your personality because they offer the highest possible returns with the most risk. Emerging markets are a good place to turn, as is anything related to the NASDAQ or Russell 2000. Or perhaps you can forget about the money that's stuck and have it as a safe stash for retirement. Resolve to keep it that way and move it into reliable government-backed securities or a stable value fund. At the very least, this may please your spouse.

Is this a good time to invest in real estate? *As you read some of this, please keep in mind the year this book is being written is 2012.*

Savers: I've met a lot of people wired for saving and security, and surprisingly, many of them love real estate. Often, much of their net worth and postretirement income comes from real estate. You need to realize, though, that real estate is far more uncertain now than it was just a few years ago. Be careful about leveraging (borrowing) too much money, especially against your home equity. Also, approach real estate investment trusts (REITs) with caution. They usually come from Wall Street and, while they have good income potential, they can tie up

your money for years; if you want access, this may not
be a good option for you.

If you're going to get into real estate, you'll
have to wear the investor cap for a while. Don't
jump in. See a number of properties, do your
homework, get to know the local market, and
bide your time. Tend toward keeping your money
accessible and favor a slow stream of regular
income over setting yourself up to take a big hit.

Investors: In spite of—or, rather, because
of—the current real estate woes, this may be the
perfect time for you to enter the mix. With all the
residential and commercial foreclosures, there's a
lot of available property to research and consider.
Still, always tread cautiously. You might do well
to learn about real estate options. Basically, you
contract with a would-be seller to buy the property
under certain conditions. You pay a premium to
lock in the price, but the extra time spent checking
the property out can make it worthwhile.

Look into websites featuring foreclosed
properties. Most are reliable, but sometimes there
are hidden problems with the properties. Don't rush
into anything (not that you usually do), and have a
good real estate lawyer on hand to check over all
the details before you finalize anything.

Speculators: You should be foaming at the mouth!
There's a ton of inventory, with most everyone
looking to sell. Today's real estate woes provide

a buyer's market if ever there was one. And with banks holding so much property, now's a good time to make some banker friends. Contact significant local property owners, too. Many of them are eager to stop dealing with renters (most people I meet who own rental property tell me today's renters are more difficult than ever to deal with) and may be looking to unload properties to leave the world of hassle. Rental property owners might be glad to see you, and they may be willing to finance the deal themselves if the property is paid off. Get out there and make some offers.

Don't overlook websites featuring foreclosed properties, either. You'll have to show some restraint over your impulsive nature. Vet properties carefully and work with a good real estate lawyer. Sometimes there are back taxes owed or other concealed problems.

How much of my investments should be liquid (easily accessible)?

First, let me explain something about the term "liquidity." Liquid assets (liquidity) are those investments which are "immediately" accessible without loss of principal and/or interest. In most cases, the more interest a financial institution is willing to pay you for your money, the less liquid that money will be to you. It is a trade-off.

For example, a savings account paying 0% interest at your local bank is completely liquid; you give the bank your money and they let you take it from them any time you wish without penalty. This makes sense because the bank—which is in the business of loaning your money to others so they can collect interest on the loan—can't depend on having your money in the long-term since it is officially in a liquid savings account. If liquidity is something you need, and you like the safety and security of the bank, you can take it up a notch by purchasing a certificate of deposit (CD). Basically, a CD has a time commitment whereby you agree to leave your money in the bank for a certain length of time, usually from 30 days up to five years. The longer period of time you agree to leave your money in the bank, the more they can depend on the interest they will make on your money, thus the more interest they will pay you for the use of it. So a one-year CD may pay 1%, while a 5-year CD could pay 2%. The longer your commitment to banks and other institutions, the more they will pay you for the "use of your money." The same holds true for insurance companies offering annuities. The longer the term of the surrender charge, the higher the interest they are willing to pay you. The more interest you desire to receive from them on the use of your money, the more penalty they will apply to that money, should you wish to take the money from them before the prescribed time period ends.

Liquidity for Savers: This is difficult because there are so many individual factors to consider. My basic suggestion for savers is to make sure you have immediate access to enough money to live for at least one year without having to spend down other assets —having to tap into a 401(k) to live on, for instance. Here's what you do; simply sit down and add up all expenses for the past year. You'll be surprised how much money you can go through in the course of a year, so don't forget anything. A small list of items may include mortgage payments, car payments, loan payments, insurance premiums, tuition fees, utilities, and other bills such as grocery and shopping expenses . . . all of it. If it comes to $40,000, you should have ready access to at least that much. Also, don't forget upcoming major expenditures that are possible, home repairs, car replacement, etc.

For savers, the savings account at the local bank will do nicely, but there are alternatives. Cash value inside a life insurance policy is very liquid and can count as "liquid" money; however, cash value in life insurance is best left untouched unless it's really an emergency, because the policy can be negatively affected when you take the money out, especially if you don't have a plan to pay it back. Penalty-free withdrawals from an annuity, T-bills, and even a box full of cash in the vegetable drawer are possibilities. And don't laugh at the last one; you'd be surprised how many people are stashing cash in the strangest places.

Beyond the $40,000—or whatever your figure is—it's mostly a matter of what makes you most comfortable. With the uncertainty of the times today, I meet savers who want all of their money—aside from money designated for retirement—liquid. How uncertain you feel about the economy, your job, your spouse's job, family situations, big-ticket items on the horizon, and other factors all influence the decision. The bottom line: don't fall for the guilt-trip gospel of the financial world telling you to avoid earning 0% on your money. For savers, sometimes zero is your friend. In fact, most savers would rather protect their principal, enjoy liquidity, and sleep at night as opposed to putting their money at risk and losing it. If you feel better knowing your money is in low-interest areas but it's always there when you need it, go with it.

Liquidity for Investors: Depending on the times, investors often take a different approach to liquidity than do savers. When things are not going well economically, investors may tend to feel better by putting funds on the sidelines in lower-interest accounts in order to stay liquid. The reason is that they want to remain flexible and ready to move on investment opportunities as they see the tide turning. investors are not likely to stay on the sidelines for long, however; they are more likely to "time" things, moving in and out of various investments as they believe things will occur. Again, for the investor, it is all about feeling in control of one's destiny, and that sometimes requires liquidity.

For instance, I met a true investor several years ago who, toward the end of the stock market gains of 2007, pulled most of his money out of the market for fear that we were in for a correction. He was correct in his timing; as we all know, the market took a plunge in 2008. He said he put the money in a money market until such time as he thought the market would return to its high of 2007. Then, as he put it, "I went looking for good buys and needed ready cash to buy."

Investors, in my opinion, should always consider having a decent percent of their overall net worth in liquid form. Why? Because you never know what may come your way . . . either good or bad. Just look at what happened following the tragic events of 9/11. Can you imagine having all of your money in the market when this uncertain event occurred? Keep in mind, the market closed! If you had needed money, you couldn't have gotten to it. And, even when the market reopened, who knew what the value of the stocks in your portfolio would be? Also, to have liquidity is prudent, if for no other reason than to be ready for the next great new investment opportunity. This doesn't mean you have to dump money in a bank account to earn nothing. There are more creative ways to maintain liquid capital. For example, the equity in your home can be a good source. Hear me out.

Let's say you have taken our free test and confirmed that you are definitely an investor. You have most of your market in illiquid, long-term investments, yet you do wish to have access to money without risk of loss. Where can you turn? Your home. Like I said, hear me out.

Let's say you recently had your home appraised for $300,000, the fair market value. You currently have a first mortgage of $100,000. Since you have the mortgage on a 30-year basis, the payments are minimal and are easily affordable to you. Other than a $300 monthly car payment, you have no other debt. So what does this scenario have to do with a liquid account? Everything—because the very liquidity you desire (without having to give the money to the bank at little or no benefit to you) is right before your very eyes . . . it is buried in the equity of your home!

In the example above, there is approximately $200,000 of equity available to you ($300,000-$100,000 = $200,000). That's $200,000 of "your" money in the equity of "your" home. The money is liquid and "tax-free" to boot. Of course, it wouldn't be wise to borrow the full equity of $200,000, but still, to borrow $50,000 in the event of an emergency or even for an investment opportunity will work. Again, this strategy of using one's home equity in such a manner may not be suitable for savers. That's because savers generally like to have a "paid for" home as one of their main goals.

Liquidity for the Speculator: I know, I know . . .
you hate letting any money sit in a savings or
checking account. It does relieve some stress though,
and can even help keep you disciplined. More
importantly, if you want to continue speculating, you
need a stash of money that's off limits to you for the
time being. I've known speculators who don't set
things up this way, and eventually there's a downturn
and they regret it.

Also, ditch the credit cards. Not because I doubt
you'll make your payments; mostly, I'm afraid you
might start using them to speculate with if the need
arises, and that's a dangerous practice. If you're not
willing to go card-free, at least set a low limit of
maybe $2,000 with the card company.

Consider this strategy: any time you make
money, take 10% off the top and put it in a savings
account. Make sure your spouse or someone else
who cares about you knows about the account
and holds you accountable for it. Commit to not
touching this money, unless it's for something truly
important. And no, more pork bellies don't count.
If you're successful at this strategy, you can move
some money to places with a little more growth
potential, like fixed annuities or stable value ETFs,
but don't try to hit a home run with it.

In terms of the strategy described above for
investors and home equity, you may be the type
to borrow a great deal of your equity. Just be
careful, as this is how so many people got into

trouble—borrowing all of their equity against an arbitrary appraised value.

How much of my investments should be guaranteed by insurance or some sort of backing?

Savers: The majority of your money should be guaranteed! That's because savers hate losing money. The only way to prevent it is by having your principal and earnings guaranteed to never go down. Despite what you may hear from the talking heads in the world of finance, there's no reason for a true saver to leave the comfort of safety and certainty for risk and uncertainty. For guaranteed investments, there are three primary kinds of financial institutions you can work with: banks with FDIC coverage; the federal government, via government bonds and bills; and insurance companies that offer guaranteed insurance contracts in fixed products such as fixed annuities and permanent cash value life insurance.

Let's start with banks. Banks are a great place to keep and "store" your money. You take comfort in knowing your money is in a brick-and-mortar location you can see, enter, and find a real person to interact with. Just be careful of what I call the "down the hall move." That's when you walk into the bank and hand the teller a check for $20,000 (you just received an inheritance, for instance, or something else providing a windfall of cash) and she suggests you consider investing in something for a "higher return" on your money. The nice employee points you in the direction of an even nicer employee "down the hall." Unbeknownst to you, that person "down the hall" usually represents Wall Street, meaning the products they will be discussing will be risky—you could lose money. The Wall Street representative down the hall may even scoff at safe banking and is adept at convincing you to change your financial plan, introducing unnecessary risk. Remember that the folks at the bank don't always represent "safe" products. Be sure to confirm which side they're on. Rule of thumb: behind the teller window is safe territory; down the hall . . . be careful!

The next safe haven can be the government. I know it's hard to think of Uncle Sam as a financial institution, but he is. Basically, other than taxing us to death, the government lives on borrowed funds . . . called government bonds. Basically, the government borrows money from the general public and then spends it on projects that are—in theory, anyway—good for Americans. The military, roads, schools, heck . . . even every flush of the toilet reminds us of our hard-earned money at work. In exchange for lending our money to the government in the form of bonds, we earn interest from them, just like we do from banks and insurance companies. Our hope is that they can pay us back; which they usually do, since all they have to do is raise taxes and/or raise our utility bills to cover the note.

Government bonds and treasury bills (T-bills), even municipal bonds, are smart picks for savers. You aren't going to get rich off these products, but you should be able to keep pace with inflation. To learn more about government bonds, check out http://treasurydirect.org/.

Insurance companies are proven safe. Stick with those that have, A minus "excellent" or better from AM Best rating service. Check ratings at http://www.ambest.com/. Even during the Great Depression in the 1930s, insurance companies all stayed afloat. Insurance companies are required to maintain much higher capital reserves than other institutions, and they have to follow very stringent rules to ensure they can fulfill all contracts with policyholders. There is security because, unlike with most investments, when you give an insurance company your money (for annuities, permanent life insurance, etc.), you receive a contract that cannot be altered or taken away from you.

Investors: You won't generally consider safe investments to be working for you the way you like. Guaranteed investments serve one main purpose for you: a safety net in the event of major losses. For you, the best way to go about it is to crunch some numbers and decide how much of your money you can handle leaving safely on the sidelines, and how much you can afford to invest. Stash the money you want guaranteed with banks, the government, and/or insurance companies. Read the summaries of these three institutions above in the response for savers. Forget the popular "rule of 100," which says there is a simple rule of how much you should have in stocks, which becomes less as you get older. Following the rule of 100, you take 100 and subtract your age from it; the resultant sum would be the maximum amount (percentage) of your portfolio you should have exposed to market risks under the rule of 100. I've met people in their eighties who, based on the rule of 100, should only have a small percent of their money in the stock market, but who have instead all their money in the market and feel fine with that. (The rule of 100, that you should have less in the market as you get older, since you have less time on this earth, is based on a faulty theory pitched by Wall Street). A true investor doesn't base how much of something to invest in by some arbitrary, one-size-fits-all rule of thumb cooked up by someone in a three-piece suit who supposedly knows best. A true investor will invest as he sees fit based, on his financial personality.

Speculators: I started putting together an in-depth response, but never mind. All I can say is, please stick at least 10% of your winnings (gains, income, or whatever) in a safe place. I know you're saying to yourself, "Isn't Tony just doing what he said the rest of the financial world is doing, cooking up arbitrary formulas as to how much to have in certain places?" The only reason I suggest putting

10% away in a safe place is to give others who may
be depending on you some peace of mind. Also,
while I know your personality never sees the glass
as half empty, it still is a fact that your speculative
activity could result in total losses. I've seen this
happen to me. So why not have just a small portion
of your money stashed away in a safe account,
just in case? Park the money in one or more of the
following: CDs, money markets, fixed insurance
contracts, or a solid ETF with low fees. The money
should be, in your mind, for retirement or for the
proverbial rainy day.

Are exchange-traded funds (ETFs) right for me?

Savers: If you decide to invest somewhere besides
the guaranteed options discussed in the previous
question, ETFs are a good way to go with a small
percentage of your assets. With other accounts, you
pay maybe 1.5% off the top to a fund manager and
another 1% to your financial advisor. They make
money whether your account goes up or down, but
you take a serious hit, as the graph illustrates. With
ETFs, you skip all the guesswork of picking the
"right" stocks or bonds. The fee is so low because
you're not paying someone to make predictions
for you—that's a service you don't need. You
buy a whole group of stocks and let it ride. Know
going in, though, that ETFs can plummet in value
like any stock or growth mutual fund. Still, ETFs
are much simpler and involve considerably lower

fees and taxes, all of which should appeal to your personality.

Investors: I'd say the same to you as I said to the savers above. Only, you should get on the research and comfortably put more than a small percentage of your assets into ETFs. They have an additional advantage for your personality, too; unlike mutual funds, which are sold at the close of the day, ETFs trade like stocks at any time. Watch out for commission costs when trading or selling. Head over to https://www.schwab.com/ and https://vanguard.com for great information on ETFs.

Speculators: Read over what I've said to the savers and investors. While ETFs won't sound too exciting to you, I'd recommend you check out the websites and consider these funds. They can be structured with puts and calls and otherwise be made to suit your personality.

Should I pay off my home mortgage early?

A lot of people assume paying off their home mortgage early is a good idea. Let me start with three compelling rebuttals:

1. The equity in your home is your money. There are only three ways to get it back: borrow against it (which you must pay back, on the bank's terms), take out a very

expensive reverse mortgage if you're at least 62 years old, or sell the home. And that last one isn't always easy these days.

2. With a home mortgage—especially one with a 30-year term—you have the bank's money locked in, so you know exactly what your cost will be. Where else can you lock in an interest rate for 30 years? You can't, unless you take a home loan.

3. With few things to deduct off your taxes, the home interest deduction can be a valuable planning tool. I like to refer to it as living in government-subsidized housing, since the government is allowing you to reduce the cost of your loan by way of the interest deduction. Of course, with all the recent changes in the tax laws, be sure to confirm whether your interest on a home loan is deductible or not.

Savers: You don't like owing money to anyone. I get that. But times have changed since those simpler days when paying off your home was the ultimate goal. I'd definitely recommend savers avoid "bad debt" on items that go down in value, like cars and other depreciating assets. But the debt on your home can sometimes be "good debt." Debt on a home isn't necessarily to be avoided, as long as you have a professional look at how it relates to your personal situation. Still, as a saver, I know all too well the feeling of having your home paid for by retirement and the fact that a paid-for home definitely gives you a more manageable cash-flow position to plan for retirement. So for savers, if you are on the fence about whether to work on getting the home paid for as soon as possible, go with your gut and get it paid off as soon as you can. None of the savers I've worked with (thousands of them over the years) has ever regretted paying off a home mortgage.

Investors: With your capacity for figuring things out, you should live according to the "cost of money" concept. Every dollar you borrow frees up a dollar of your own money to invest. If you take out a home loan at 5% interest for 30 years, you have the bank's money locked up for that time. No matter what happens to future interest rates, the bank must honor the 5% rate—your cost of money. Assuming you can deduct the interest from your taxes, the government effectively lowers your cost of money. Then, if you reinvest those savings and make more than your new cost of money, you win! Investors should pay off "bad debt" on things that go down in value. However, they should take their time paying off "good debt" on their home.

Speculators: You probably haven't even considered paying off your home. There's no reason to lock up all that money, right? You love OPM (other people's money) and realize that by using the bank's low-interest money via a home loan, you can do wonders with it. My advice to speculators is to follow your heart, yet I would remind you to be careful with your debt-to-equity ratios—which is what got everybody in trouble with our latest mortgage crisis. You should try to keep equity in your home of at least 30% of the home's fair market value. In other words, even though I know it is tempting to max out a loan against your home, avoid the temptation. If your home is worth $200,000, keep the home loan to no more than $140,000. If you are married, consider the fact that your spouse (assuming he or she is not a speculator) may feel most comfortable if you have a plan of action to pay the home off, just for your spouse's peace of mind.

Should I liquidate my 401(k) or IRA to pay off debt?

For years, I've cohosted a live call-in TV show on Louisville NBC affiliate, WAVE3 TV, answering a whole host of questions regarding a wide range of financial matters. Recently, with the downturn of the economy, more and more callers are asking if they should use retirement accounts to pay off debt. Depending on your financial personality, here's my take on this matter.

Savers: The 401(k) and traditional IRA, once considered the sacred cows of the financial world, now appear to be a new option for Americans to climb out of debt. Cashing in the forbidden fruit of a pre-tax retirement account can be a viable option for people trying to get out from behind the eight ball. It's worth consideration as it is certainly a sign of the changing times we are in. Still, be sure you first verify the taxes owed should you decide to take this option.

Investors: You understand cause and effect, that when you do something in one place, it can have consequences somewhere else. Take a look at the explanation I just gave the savers about how liquidating an IRA to pay off debt can affect your tax situation. You can probably come up with better ways to create cash flow to pay down your debt. Other options might include refinancing your existing home to a lower interest rate, or even a 30 year mortgage. You might even consider reducing your contribution to your existing 401k. Both options will improve immediate cash flow so you can attack the debt more quickly.

Also, think about the cost-of-money issue again. If the earnings on your qualified accounts are as high as or higher than the interest on your loans, leave the qualified accounts alone and don't get too hung up on the debt. However, if your debt is becoming unmanageable, action may become necessary, either in the form of liquidation or another solution.

Speculators: I know, I know . . . liquidating a 401(k) or IRA to pay off debt is probably the furthest thing from your mind. You probably don't even have a 401(k) or much money in one of these qualified accounts, nor should you. If you do have a considerable amount in a qualified account, consider drawing it out gradually over time to move it to more tax-friendly vehicles that you have more control over.

If you decide to liquidate a qualified account, make sure you know ahead of time how it will affect your tax situation. Read the example I wrote in my response to this question for savers. Taxes aside, someone with your money personality certainly won't miss the 401(k)/IRA when it's gone.

What amount and type of life insurance is right for me?

Savers: Your desire to preserve and protect your hard-earned money extends to passing along your accumulations to your family when you're gone. Life insurance is a significant consideration, especially because it's the only asset guaranteed to be passed along to your heirs on a "tax-free" basis at an amount greater than what you contributed. That should appeal to every saver.

Look into purchasing a good amount of permanent life insurance, such as whole life or universal life insurance. If you choose term life, you won't have many planning options for how to use, enjoy, and protect your money in retirement. Plus, term life is so cheap because you're probably never going to collect on it. Owning permanent life insurance is the key to a worry-free retirement because it gives you permission to spend other assets, knowing that when you die, money will go to your loved ones tax-free and free of probate.

If you're younger and can't afford permanent life insurance, purchase term life insurance in an amount that's at least 20 times more than your annual income. Later down the line, gradually convert to whole life or guaranteed universal life insurance. This gets your money back, either while you're still alive or for your heirs. Make sure first that your policy allows you to convert it without having to go through all the underwriting.

Investors: Your predilection for studying, organizing, and growing money will push you to minimize your insurance premiums, and with them your lost opportunity costs, or LOCs. This is usually a smart instinct, but not where life insurance is concerned.

Since interest rates spiked back in the early 1980s, people have had it drilled into them that term life is cheap and the best way to go, and that whole life is too expensive to be worthwhile. This is bad advice.

There's only one true economic certainty that requires no research and that has stood the test of time: we all die. Given this fact, why would you so hastily rule out the only insurance product that guarantees tax-free build-up of money, easy access to it at little or no cost, a tax-free death benefit that can be leveraged through some fairly unique planning, and avoidance of income taxes and probate?

Check out http://leapsystems.com/ and http://infinitebanking.org/ to read about the advantages of whole life insurance. Once you look into it, it should be very attractive to your personality. For the younger investors out there who can't afford permanent life insurance, read over my advice to young savers above. It applies to you, too.

Speculators: I knew a speculator who told me that before he had a wife and kid, life insurance was the farthest thing from his mind. Premiums would just be a waste of money.

Later, when he married and had his first child, his perception changed. He realized others depended on his ability to make money. While he continued to speculate, he backed off a little. He purchased term life insurance, which is probably the best choice for his personality, in an amount of $250,000. I asked him how he came up with the amount. He replied, "I don't know, just seemed like plenty to me."

So then I asked him this question: What if I handed you $250,000 cash now (you should have seen his eyes light up) in exchange for you agreeing to pay me all your winnings for the rest of your life? As you can probably imagine, he wasn't too enthused.

That's basically what he was setting his family up for upon his death. After I explained that, he immediately locked in another $1,000,000 on himself and $500,000 on his wife.

Should I invest in an annuity for retirement? If so, what type?

First, let me offer brief explanations of the four basic types of annuities: fixed-interest annuities, variable annuities, fixed indexed annuities, and immediate annuities. Annuities are issued and underwritten by insurance companies.

Fixed-interest annuity: This is a contract whereby you give your money to an insurance company and are guaranteed a fixed rate of interest for one or more years. What they pay you is generally based on the return of the company's investment portfolio, but you get the guaranteed rate regardless of their profitability or loss. It's similar to the way a bank CD works.

Let's say you give the insurance company $100,000, and they promise you 4% interest the first year of the contract. At the end of the year, they add $4,000 to your account. The $104,000 is the new floor on your account. If they agreed to pay you 3% (assuming the annuity's interest rate adjusts every year, but some annuities offer multiple-year rate guarantees) in the second year, it applies to this new floor. ($104,000 x 3%). The process repeats annually until your contract ends and you either withdraw your annuity money or select a new annuity contract from the same insurance company.

Variable annuity: Your money is invested in mutual funds or some other type of security. Although you have unlimited upside potential and can make a lot of money in a variable annuity, you also have unlimited downside and can lose a lot of money. Over the past several years, you might have experienced or seen market losses. I have personally witnessed variable annuity losses of up to 50%! Such losses were no doubt suffered by some people who could ill afford to lose that much of their retirement savings.

Fixed indexed annuity: These annuities were first offered in the go-go 1990s. I remember insurance companies calling on me to sell them. At that time, with many of my clients making huge returns in the stock market, I had no interest in selling these products, because they limit or cap the rate of return.

For instance, say you purchase a fixed indexed annuity with a 40% participation rate. If the stock market goes up 10% that year, that means you would earn 4% (10% x 40% = 4%). While you aren't taking a "position in the market," your earnings are "linked" to the market. The insurance company is not investing your money in the stock market, but is using your money for their normal investments, including buying bonds. But since you are paid earnings based on the market, they hedge their risk by offering you "market-linked" returns. Hedging can get rather technical, so suffice it to say they are buying "risk insurance" to ensure they can pay you the promised return whether the market goes up, down, or sideways.

Let's say your fixed indexed annuity contract offers a 40% participation rate and during the year the actual stock market index you have selected, say the S&P 500, goes up 20%. You would receive credit for only 40% of this 20% gain in the market. This equals 8% (because .4 x.2 =.08). So, if you placed $100,000 with the insurance company, you would make $8,000 during the year, and this amount would be added to your account. Obviously, this isn't as good as a variable annuity that would earn the full 20% that year, or $20,000, minus fees.

But wait . . . let's say the market lost 20% instead of making 20%. What's the return on the variable annuity? Unfortunately, you'd be down the full amount plus fees. No doubt you'd be unhappy. A reading of the variable annuity's prospectus tells you the variable annuity has no floor and you can lose big time in a bad market. What about the fixed indexed annuity? In this case, if the market nosedives, your $108,000 is locked in. You wouldn't lose a penny. Plus, next year, if the market goes back up, you ride back up with it, starting from $108,000 and adding to your previous gains.

Be aware that indexed annuities are gaining in popularity, with more and more inexperienced agents selling these products. Don't confuse the "income rider" rate of returns with what the actual "contract value" can earn. As of the date of this book, the "contract value" returns will be much lower than in the past. That's because insurance company bond yields have fallen, meaning they can't pay as high of participation rates and caps as they have paid in the past. Many agents, anxious to sell these, don't understand this fact. My suggestion: ask the agent to assume the "contract value" is growing at no more than 3%, just to be more realistic.

Immediate annuity: An immediate annuity is like a pension. You give your money to the insurance company in exchange for a lifetime income for a set number of years or for the life of your beneficiary. The insurance company then estimates the life expectancy of an individual or the median life expectancy of a group of like people, e.g., those of the same age or gender. That determines how much income you'll receive for the period of time selected. The goal is to guarantee a dependable stream of money.

The main problem with immediate annuities is that once they are set up, they usually can't be changed. It's possible to change any other annuity into an immediate annuity by "annuitizing," or taking your balance over a number of years or over your lifetime in periodic payments. An annuity with a "lifetime income benefit rider" can be turned into a lifetime income, but this type of annuity has a lot more flexibility than an immediate annuity with respect to changing your mind and taking a lump sum partial withdrawal or giving up the income and taking all your money out in a lump sum.

Now that you've digested all that, below is my personality-based advice.

Savers: For someone who hates losing money, annuities—and especially fixed annuities—are a safe, secure, perfect investment for retirement. The fixed interest rate annuity, as noted, is like a CD and is well suited to your personality. Fixed indexed annuities are a good deal. Definitely look into these, particularly if they include an income rider. You may also appreciate an immediate annuity for its pensionlike qualities. Savers should stay away from variable annuities, though.

Investors: The many types of annuities offer fertile research ground. Remember, annuities aren't about beating the stock market; they're about providing a steady stream of income in retirement. Any type of annuity could work for you, though fixed interest annuities are probably least appealing. Variable annuities have good growth potential with no current tax liability. You just have to be okay riding the ups and downs of the stock market. A fixed indexed annuity is a good deal for gaining from the market without the risk. Always figure out the exact fees you may incur. Download the Free Annuity Fee Sheet on my site (http://www.tonywalkerfinancial. com/). Have your advisor complete it and give it back to you to facilitate disclosure.

Speculators: Annuities aren't for you. If you want to save some money for a rainy day, then sure, go ahead and buy one. You'll be most interested in the variable annuity.

Should I invest in gold, silver, or other commodities and or futures?

Savers: In today's uncertain economic times, people hear more and more about buying gold and other commodities. These are very risky investments. Who even knows that gold will be valuable following a total economic collapse? People seem to buy gold mostly because they don't know what else to do in preparation for a worst-case scenario. That's not really a compelling reason to do it. I spoke to someone in the gold and silver business recently. He recommends that concerned people buy $10,000 in silver because its smaller denomination makes it easier to trade, as compared to the more expensive gold.

If savers want to purchase gold, silver, or other commodities, I won't tell them not to. Just know going in that it's highly speculative. Don't start selling off your belongings to acquire gold. And if you're not too keen on stacking gold bullion in the closet, consider putting on the investor's cap for a little while and looking into gold indexes and other gold-type funds.

Investors: Seems like there's been a sort of gold rush on gold lately, doesn't it? Remember the basic principles . . . when everyone's buying something, it might be a good time to sell it. Think about whether you're buying gold as a short-term position or as a buy-and-hold prospect. As an investor, you can profit from the current high the precious metal is experiencing. Like all investments, it will hit a peak, and it may happen sooner than you think. Try not to follow the herd on this one. Be creative and look to take advantage of the possibility of falling prices. If you are going to get into gold, consider gold ETFs for the flexibility to hedge your bets and potential losses if the market plunges.

Speculators: If you aren't rushing to bet against all the people clamoring to buy gold right now, there must be something wrong with you. Everyone's buying it. Surely you see opportunity in doing the opposite. Go with your gut, put some money on the line, and bet against them all. We both know prices, which are being artificially inflated by ridiculous demand, won't continue on their current trajectory.

As I wrote this, just days ago, Superstorm Sandy unleashed its fury on the Northeast. Millions are without power, and there is no way of getting gasoline to them. With that said, you'd think (or at least it seems that way in my simple/saver mind) that if I were a bettin' man I'd bet that prices of gasoline in the region (and across the country, for that matter, as a result of this storm) would skyrocket, right? The answer is; maybe, maybe not.

You see, while savers and investors alike sit, watch, and wait to see the aftereffects of this terrible damage, speculators are busy trying to "bet" on which way gas prices will move; this is called *oil futures.* One speculator is betting the future price of gas will actually go down (he is speculating that people cannot use the gas anyway (as many cars and roads were destroyed), so the demand will go down, thus lowering the need for supply, thus lowering gas prices); another speculator thinks gas prices will go up for the opposite reasons, so he bets the other way. And don't think these speculators are dummies just throwing good money after bad. The majority of speculators are highly intelligent, competitive people who want to win and win big. Think I'm kidding? Below is what someone in the gas futures market is looking at and studying. See if you know what the heck this stuff is all about:

> Natural Gas Futures: $1.50 per MMBtu ($15,000 per contract) for the first two months. Initial back month limits of $0.15 (15¢) per MMBtu rise to $0.30 (30¢) per MMBtu if the previous day's settlement price in any back month is at the $0.15

(15¢) limit. In the event of a $0.75 (75¢)
per MMBtu move in either of the first
two contract months, limits on all months
become $0.75 per MMBtu in all months
from the limit in place in the direction of the
move.

And you thought those mutual fund statements
were difficult to understand!

Conclusion

The 3 Personalities of Money, this unique concept of mind over money, is a warning shot over the financial bow. I trust you agree that following the one size fits all mantra of the financial world is not always the best path; rather, at some point in your life, you will need to step away from all the noise so you can discover who you are, how you're wired, and what's best for you, rather than for them. This is what differentiates The 3 Personalities of Money from all other financial theories about money, and yes, even psychology and behavioral finance.

So what's next?

If you haven't taken the free 3-minute test to determine your financial personality, do so now by logging on to 3Personalities.com. Take advantage of this scientifically proven test so you can immediately make better financial decisions. As illustrated throughout this book, new insight into your financial personality gives you permission to follow your predominant financial personality, to satisfy your built-in desire to save, invest, or speculate.

In addition to reading this book and taking the free online test, another positive action step you can take is to study the real-life stories found at the end of this book. These stories, which are of actual people I personally interviewed while researching this project, will force you to consider "your" reaction to "their" responses to a wide variety of financial scenarios. These stories will assist you in finding out more about yourself and how that self responds to the personal responses of others, the "why" we do what we do, so you can begin understanding more about your unique personality. You will get confirmation that there is no one-size-fits-all response to these stories. The more you begin to relate other situations to your responses, the more you will learn about yourself.

Remember, the overall goal of this book, the free test, and the stories is not to put you in a financial personality box, but simply to help you learn more about this powerful concept of mind over money in action, in hopes that you'll be more confident and worry less about money. As you learn more about your financial personality and the financial products and strategies related to it, you'll see matters in a new and more confident light. You will approach savings and investments in ways that make sense and make you feel good about what you're doing.

Besides taking the free financial personality test and reviewing the stories, what else can you do? At the very end of the book is a brief list of helpful websites and articles geared toward all three financial personalities. So whether you are a saver, an investor, or speculator, you can find more information to assist you. Believe me, there's much more where this came from! Take advantage of the Internet—it's *free,* for goodness sake—and begin the journey of discovering which investments and financial strategies mesh with who you are and what you are comfortable doing.

Embrace who you are. Embrace your financial personality. Embrace life.

Thank you for reading. Let me wish you (please select the appropriate sign-off for your personality):

a. *Happy Saving!*

b. Happy *Investing!*

c. *Happy Speculating!*

Real-life Financial Stories to Help You Explore Your Financial Personality

The 3 Personalities of Money project has been in the making for years. When I first began the painstaking task of organizing this, I interviewed a wide group of people who had varying degrees of interest in and knowledge about money. The following are actual real-life stories, recorded and transcribed several years ago; some of the stories and the responses may seem dated, but they still matter, regardless of what current market conditions might be. These personal stories will help you in your journey, as each of them reveals just how unique and different we all are when it comes to different situations and experiences regarding money. It may serve you well to read them at your leisure. How you relate to the world around you is a good indicator of how you are wired financially. Looking at things from others' perspectives will require you to be more introspective about your own personality.

I would suggest reading a few stories, thinking about them, and recording your responses. Put the book down and pick it up later if you wish. Pick it up again and read a few more. Remember, this is a journey of discovery and confirmation as to who you are and how you're wired for money. "Mind over money" is new and refreshing, but old habits are hard to break. You will be tempted to drift away from your predominant personality and into the other worlds. Be careful. Stay focused, keep learning; there are no right and wrong answers, just a lack of understanding of financial personalities from the financial world and lack of knowledge about what is best suited for you. It is up to you to take control of your money.

Although this exploration is in no way scientific, these real-life stories will further allow you to explore more about your financial personality as it relates to others and what they may be thinking, further proof that one size does not fit all.

The Death of Uncle Charlie

Several months ago I was notified by letter that a long-lost uncle named Charlie had passed away and had included me in his will. I, along with several other nieces and nephews, would be *receiving a check for each of our share of Charlie's estate. Little did anyone know (or care during that time) how much the land he owned. Last week, the UPS guy pulls up in my driveway and hands me an overnight envelope from the attorney handling Uncle Charlie's estate. My share: $800,000! To be honest, I'm scared to death . . . . I've never had that kind of money. In fact, I haven't even cashed the check. It's sitting in my dresser drawer, just under the socks. My wife says I should put it in the bank. A close friend, who is really good with money, says I should invest it. Heck, I've worked at a factory all my life . . . . never had any money to speak of . . . I don't know what to do. My gut feeling is to shop around with banks and buy a bunch of certificates of deposit from different banks and live off whatever interest they will pay me. I don't want to lose any of this money and banks are FDIC insured.*

How do you relate?

a. If I had such a windfall of money, I'd hate to lose any of it too. The idea of CDs and being FDIC insured makes sense to me.

b. To me, this is found money—money I never planned on having anyway, so why not enjoy it or at least try to invest it for growth?

c. I can relate to the fear of having responsibility of something I never thought about. My first step would be to find a good financial advisor and turn the money over to him.

d. I'd book a plane to Vegas.

Hanging in There for Now

I'm five years away from retirement. I work as an assistant principal at a high school. It is getting busier and busier at work as my workload never seems to get any easier. I used to keep up with stocks and bonds . . . mutual funds within my 401(k) plan . . . did all my own research. But these days, I'm putting money into the stock market without doing as much research as I used to do. I'd like to, but I just don't have the time, energy, and interest I once did. I do think the next five years will be good for the stock market as I think we are going to come out of this recession. In fact, I'd like to put more into international stocks if I just had the time to research them. I just wish somebody would help me take care of my portfolio and manage it for me—I would feel better about that. I feel pretty nervous about all of my money in the stock market, but I guess I'll just hang in there for now.

How do you relate?

a. I feel the same way as the narrator, in that the stock market is the only place I know of where you can get growth.

b. I can't relate to her at all. Why not play it safe at this point in life?

c. To me, if she is that close to retirement, wouldn't it make more sense to avoid risk at all cost?

Avoiding the Spending Trap

There's an old saying that when something catches your eye, you better start saving for it rather than figuring out how you can finance it. Problem was, by the time I got the money saved to buy something, I would discover that I really didn't want it anymore. In a way, this line of thinking helped protect me from buying things I really didn't need anyway. I decided to put all my money in the bank and assume the money would be available to me down the road. I didn't worry about all the interest I was making, or losing, depending on your perspective, I just kept saving, and that saved me from the impulse to buy. I never have fallen into the trap of spending money. I don't like risking it either. All that worry over money ain't worth it. It just gets you into trouble.

How do you relate?

a.   I can relate to and agree with this.

b.   Where did you find this guy?

c.   I don't save money like this, yet what he says make sense.

Mid Fifties and Falling

All I feel like I am doing is watching the stock market fall and when the stock market falls, my money is falling, too. I am in my mid fifties. I mean, what else am I supposed to do? I have been told you are supposed to keep all of your money in the market, but it just feels like my whole world is falling apart. I feel like I have made a bad decision—that I don't know what to do. Here's the bad part; nobody else seems to want to take responsibility with me. I need $5,000 a month . . . after taxes [emphasis added]! *I've got $800,000, and while I know that sounds like a lot of money, back in 2007 it was $1.2 million! And at my age, I'm scared the money won't last. I don't know what to do with the money. Right now, I've moved a lot of it to CDs and money market accounts, just waiting to see what will happen. Everybody says now is a good time to invest in the market—that stocks are on sale. I am working at a part-time job as I was recently laid off from my full-time job. I am not in* *bad shape; I have got wonderful things going for me. I see myself as possibly one day being financially independent yet I don't know where to invest my money.*

How do you relate?

a. If I had $800,000 I would put it somewhere safe.

b. I can understand how she feels . . . she had $1.2 million and she lost money.

c. I agree with one statement: "Now is a good time to jump back in!"

Who Said Anything about Risk?

*Ever since college, I have been fine taking risks.
In fact, I have owned several businesses that have
gone broke. And every time we would claw back and
fight back; me and my wife . . . she's always been
there with me. Now, I have kids and have to support
them and play it a little safer. To me, there is nothing
wrong with taking calculated risks. The way I look
at it, as long as I stay healthy—even if I go broke—I
can always build it up again. I can get out and work
hard and provide for my family. Risk? I don't really
think in terms of risking anything, other than being
afraid to journey in areas of life that nobody else
wants to go. I mean, that's where the opportunities
lie. I guess I don't understand why everybody
wouldn't want to look at life and money this way. Life
is too short, so you might as well go for it. I say, you
don't necessarily have to be a gambler, but take risks
in life, especially when it comes to money."*

How do you relate?

a.   I like the way this guy thinks.

b.   This guy is crazy.

c.   I admire people who think like this, but I just
can't go there.

Avoiding the Tax Man

Believe it or not, one of the best investments we ever made was our whole life insurance policy, taken out years ago. I remember the guy selling it to us kept reminding us about how the dividends would one day continue to pay a reasonable amount; he talked about all these tax advantages and this huge death benefit that would come to me when my husband passed away—tax free! My husband, of course, was a bit shy about this much life insurance, but over the years what we have noticed is that the cash value and death benefit continues to grow. The death benefit provides protection for me and, in a way, has allowed my husband to continue to do things that he wants to do. He continues to enjoy work, has some real estate investment and overall, the whole life policy has helped us understand that the life insurance is actually a permission slip for us to spend and enjoy our other monies. Let's face it, we're all going to die, and this just gives us peace of mind knowing that we can leave tax-free assets to our kids. So to me, life insurance is an excellent way to set aside money for somebody like us."

How do you relate?

a. I've always been told that whole life insurance is a terrible investment!

b. I'm not worried about leaving money to anyone when I die.

c. If you're telling me that whole life insurance can guarantee me tax-free money during my life and tax-free money for my spouse and kids when I die, then count me in.

Commodities Gone Wild

Back in the early 1980s, I worked at the Chicago Mercantile Exchange as a runner. The Mercantile Exchange is a place where commodity specialists work. I worked for a livestock analyst, so I got a little bit of interest there and learned about the business, became a financial planner and really got very educated about that world—commodities. On the floor of the commodities . . . man . . . it was wild! The commodities business is so different from buying stocks. In some ways, though, it is similar. There are different types of people in the commodities business. Some of them are what we call "fundamentalists" that really monitor numbers and work hard at tracking things. They know the price of hogs, for instance, and have a good feel for what the price is going to do. They can turn this into a science. Some of them use charts, and some fly by the seat of their pants. Some base their decisions on the past and their gut feeling. But all in all, investing in commodities and being speculative with your money, you know . . . I guess you wouldn't want to put all your money there, but I think it is a good investment.

How do you relate?

a. The only hog I want to invest in is the pound of bacon at the grocery store.

b. I have never traded in commodities but the idea interests me.

c. You stick with betting on the price of hogs—I'll stick with the safe stuff.

Wasted Time and Energy

I'm five years away from retirement. I used to really keep up with stocks, bonds, and mutual funds. Did all of my own research. These days though, I'm putting money into the stock market without doing any research. I'd like to, but I just don't have the time or energy. Personally . . . I think over the next five years, the market will be fine, I mean, we're coming out of a recession, or at least that's what the experts keep saying. So if that's the case, the market should really rebound, and I don't want to miss out! Quite frankly, I'd put more money in the market if I had it. I just wish somebody would help me take care of my portfolio and manage it; I would feel a lot better about it. But, with my workload as an assistant principal, I don't even have the time to research advisors. I guess I'll just hang in there for now.

How do you relate?

a. To me, if you're that close to retirement, and you say you don't have the time to do all that research, why continue to take risk?

b. Either you're a liar or a big chicken . . . if you're so good at research and investing, why not focus on that?

c. I'd say get back in the game if you feel confident in what you are doing.

Don't Get Madoffed

I hate to admit this, but several years ago, I got caught up in a Ponzi scheme . . . at least that is what they call it. Heck, I didn't even know what a Ponzi scheme was before this happened. I'm a saver, but like a lot of folks, I thought the only way to really make money was by investing in the stock market. But . . . like I said, I really wanted to keep my money safe. What was I supposed to do? CDs paid next to nothing, and I felt I needed to do something. Along come some good friends at church. They were advisors and well known as

people providing alternatives to the stock market.
These guys were offering investments yielding 8%
and 9% (or so they said). Well, you can probably
guess the rest—there was no money going into CDs
or anything else for that matter. These clowns were
fictitiously creating statements and mailing them
to clients as if the money was really there . . . it
wasn't. I really felt like an idiot. I still have some
money but, you know, I am in my mid 40s . . . I
don't have 20 years left to just sit around and watch
the market. Everybody keeps telling me to put my
money in the market, so I guess that is what I'll do.

How do you relate?

a. With 20 years left till retirement, I'd consider
    an index fund. That way, you know where your
    money is, fees are low, and if the market races
    back up—a nice return.

b. Just one more reason I don't want anything to
    do with stock market or those representing it. I
    say play it safe.

c. Just because someone at church says to invest
    in a CD doesn't mean you should flee to safety.
    The market isn't for chickens, but for people
    that know and understand risks.

Fill 'er Up?

*There is an old saying, when something catches
your eye and you think you want it, you'd better
start saving money to purchase it rather than goin'
out and financin' it. Well, by the time I would get
my money saved to buy somethin', here is what I
discovered, I didn't really want it; and, in a way
that helped protect me from spending money, that
in some cases, I didn't have anyway. I decided
to put my money in the bank and assume that
money would be safer that way and also would be
available to me down the road. I really don't like
worrying about all this stuff that you can't control.
I mean, who knows what interest rates will do in
the future and what the stock market may be one
day. To me, it makes a lot more sense to keep saving
money instead of always buying stuff on impulse.
My advice, save like hell and play it safe.*

How do you relate?

a. Sorry, fella, but I have to disagree with you on
    the finance thing. I can't imagine *not* borrowing
    money.

b. I think this is a wonderful story and one that we
    need to remind young people of.

c. Where are you finding these folks, Tony? How in the world can you ever get ahead if aren't willing to take risks?

Gallons of Gas Add Up

It was 1954 when I went to work for this fella in a service station. I was 16 at the time when the owner of the gas station told me I could fill up my car with gas anytime I wanted to. He would then put a credit card receipt in the cash register so when I got my paycheck, he would deduct the cost of the gas I used up off of my net pay. This seemed like a good idea to me, so I would get 5 gallons of gas, which in 1954 was 50 cents a gallon. I'd then put the ticket in the cash register. Well, here's the funny part, the first week that I worked with this fella, I had been buying all this gas and putting the credit tickets in the cash register without really thinking about "how much" gas I was using. So come that first Saturday evening, when it was time to get my first paycheck, my actual check for all that work was five bucks! Five bucks for a week's worth of work? I thought, what in the world . . . then I realized what happened. Since I really wasn't paying for the gas out of my pocket, I didn't pay any attention to how much gas I was using. That lesson in life taught me to never borrow money for anything, because when you're borrowing money, you're really spending money that's not yours, and you forget that there's a day of reckoning. If you want my advice, it's better to save money and pay cash for everything whenever you can.

How do you relate?

a. I'll have to admit, this story really makes sense. I appreciate the way he saved money.

b. This story proves that saving money is always better than borrowing it.

c. We're taking advice from a guy who used to pump gas? With this mentality, I bet he's still working at the gas station.

A Friend of a Friend

I've got a friend who doesn't mind taking risks. We'll just call him Harry. Now, I like saving money, but Harry is kind of a free-thinking kind of guy. He likes to read research, and one of the things he loves to talk about is the stock market. Now, me, I am not real informed of the stock market, I just don't understand it, but, Harry loves the stock market, and he loves to talk about all those times he's made money in the market. In fact, while a lot of people have lost money lately in the market, Harry's done pretty well. Me: trying to keep up with all the stock market creates problems, especially

*when it comes to keeping up with all those
statements and paperwork. But the funny thing
is that Harry never seems to talk too much about
when he's losing money. It is kind of like fishing,
you know everybody always talks about the fish, but
they don't tell you about the little one that got away.
I guess for me, I just don't have the stomach for the
ups and downs like Harry."*

How do you relate?

a. What you've got is one friend (a saver) who
doesn't understand the mind of an investor.

b. I think it's fine that the saver is apprehensive
about investing money in things he or she
doesn't understand.

c. If you don't have the stomach for it, stay home;
otherwise, quit trying to convince others to stay
out of the market.

Widow in Waiting

*I'm a widow. My husband, who was a well-known
accountant, died several years ago following a
long bout with cancer. He was a good man and
always took time to take care of all the financial
stuff. He even had a very good stockbroker
whom he suggested I meet with as soon as he*

passed. Shortly after he died, I visited with his broker to see where I stood. Keep in mind, I was a wreck emotionally. When it came to money, I never handled any of it. My husband and the stockbroker related well with all these facts, figures, and diagrams. Me: when she showed me all those statements and charts, I was lost. I tried to explain to her that I didn't understand any of the investments, but certainly wanted my money safe and protected. It was all the money I had. I couldn't go back to work. After pleading with my broker to move the money to safer territory, she reluctantly did so. Now, I'm afraid after listening to her that my money won't keep pace with inflation and that I might run out. I've got all my money in CDs, government bonds, and fixed annuities. I know I won't make much, but it's nice to know that I won't lose any of it.

How do you relate?

a. Why would a widow, who knows nothing about the market, ever invest in the market if the stockbroker can't explain it to her?

b. This widow has no business in the market. Find an advisor who focuses on safer investments and better understands the plight of widows.

c. The very fact that she is a widow and her husband was heavily in the stock market is the very reason this widow needs to step up to the plate and work with her husband's advisor. Obviously, he trusted the advisor and so should this widow.

There's an Old Saying

My Uncle used to have an old saying . . . "You spend 4 years to get a $40 watch, and you don't leave things at work." I guess that was ok for him, but for me, I love hard work. I'm 43 years old and consider myself an entrepreneur. I was a financial advisor with a well-known financial firm before going into business for myself. I love doing my own thing and am ok taking risks with my money . . . calculated risks, of course. I don't want to work "for the man" but for myself. I know my uncle hated to owe money to anybody, but hey, how are you going to make any money if you're not willing to borrow it? I've borrowed hundreds of thousands of dollars over the years, and my business has done great as a result of being able to make money on other people's money. That is how the economy works. I mean, if nobody borrowed money, the economy would come to a standstill. So far, I have been very successful. But as I get older, I'm starting to get into more of a protectionist mode. I mean, who wants to be in debt all their life? I hate to admit it, but lately, I'm starting to agree a little with my uncle.

How do you relate?

a. I admire those who take calculated risks. You're on a roll. Quit listening to the voice of your uncle.

b. I could never borrow this much money. I like your uncle's line of thinking.

c. Why should this person play it safe now when he is a born winner?

Oh, for the Good Ol' Days

Back in my younger days, I was investing in stocks. I was lucky, because the company I worked for had stock splits, which meant I was accumulating more shares the longer I worked. As a result, I was able to buy a house and put money in the 401k . . . even had a little extra money to play around with. But you know, now I am retired and on a fixed income. I have a comfortable retirement. I sure don't want to go back to work. At this point in my life, I'm nervous, having most of my retirement money in my former employer's company stock. What if they have financial troubles? But I hate to sell it. And even if I sell some of the stock, where would I put it? With interest rates so low, I hate not to earn anything on my money! We want to leave money to our kids, but what if the market tanks and we lose a lot of what we've accumulated? Right now, my philosophy: set aside money we aren't using and leave it in a safe place. At this point, I think the more you can stash away in savings right now, the better.

How do you relate?

a. This story should be a lesson to all investors that the key is to invest for the long term and not change courses, even in retirement.

b. I wouldn't call these folks investors; they're savers. I thought you were supposed to move out of stocks as you approached retirement, not stay in them.

c. I say, stay with the one who brought you to the dance. If it weren't for the company stock, he would not be in the wonderful position he is in. Hang in there with the stocks.

Should I Be Ashamed of Myself?

I used to be ashamed to say this, but I am a professional gambler. I am in my 30s now; my parents are very, very conservative, I think they even used to be a little ashamed of me for what I did, but you know what, look at all the poker guys on ESPN, I mean it's big business [emphasis added]. *Don't believe me . . . just look at all the state funding of lotteries and casinos. I figure, if they can make money, I can, too. I know how the system works, and I do believe that over time, you can beat the odds if you know what you're doing.* [pause] *Do I take risks with my money? Yeah, I guess you could say so. I mean I've lost thousands of dollars overnight, but then, wake up the next day and double my money. Gambling is based on the law of large numbers, the law of averages, you've gotta stay in the game. Think about insurance companies: they're gambling that people don't have any big claims. The more people they insure, the less likely they are to lose money, because they know not everybody's gonna have a claim. Do I think gambling is for everybody? Of course not, but to me, it doesn't bother me at all, I think if you enjoy gambling and you stay on top of it, you can work the numbers right, it could work in your favor. Heck, look at the commodities and just various exchanges out there; all they are doing is betting the other person loses. I am ok with taking risks with my money. It's actually fun!*

How do you relate?

a. I disagree. Gambling and investing in the stock market are not the same thing.
b. To me, if you don't know what you're doing in the market, you're really no different from the gambler, are you?

c.   He will do well. It's not gambling if you think you can win!

No Time Like the Present

This is the greatest time in life to be buying stocks. The Dow is below 10,000. I mean, just a few years ago, it was over 14,000, so you know it's going back up . . . it always does! I can't believe people aren't in the market. That's just crazy. People locking up their money in these 2 and 3% CDs and annuities . . . what a joke. They're just turning over their money to the banks and insurance companies and letting them make all the money just because they're afraid of losing some of their principal. And even if the market drops, somebody's always bailing out companies. Usually, the companies eventually come back. My feeling: if you've got over 10 years before you'll need the money, put it in the stock market or something that will grow. And if you're nervous about putting all of your money in the market or some other growth-oriented investment all at once, put it in over time. That way you diversify your chances of losing money. Just do it and quit watching the market so close. It always takes care of itself.

How do you relate?

a. I agree with this guy and believe the 10-year time horizon makes sense.

b. Nobody has a crystal ball, and as we've seen, the market doesn't always go up and stay up. How can you say the market always goes up?

c. I would be confident with this way of thinking. I just don't think you'll lose any money in the market over that long a period of time.

Reboot Your Personality

I'm a 29-year-old computer salesman. Currently, I work in a small retail store. I use my income from sales to cover my basic expenses. I don't put money in my 401(k) plan, but instead, put it in real estate. Years ago, my father loaned me some money to invest in a fourplex. It's been going great ever since. I love using other people's money to pay for investments. Sure, it gets old having to deal with renters, but there's tax advantages to being in real estate and I get a good income so that one day, the property will be paid for. You can't beat it! After several years of doing this, now I have no problem borrowing money from banks for more real estate. I have a good working relationship with a banker and he makes sure to keep things in check. So, again, for me, I am putting every nickel I have got into rental property, and one day, hopefully, I can continue to flip it, sell it, live off the income . . . there are so many options.

So what would I tell people: borrow every nickel you can find and start buying houses, apartments, whatever seems like a good investment and don't look back. It's like my dad always says about real estate: they ain't making any more of it.

How do you relate?

a. I love it! Here's a young man that isn't in the market but truly understands investments.

b. With all the foreclosures and potential bad renters out there, I'd be nervous about borrowing all that money.

c. Didn't Donald Trump begin his wealth-building years in real estate?

The Last of the Big Spenders

We're not big spenders. I wouldn't call us frugal, but we don't overspend. We buy what we can afford and the things we can't afford, we just don't buy them. With investments, I am one of those that likes to play it safe. We have a small percent in growth mutual funds and a few shares of stock my father left me, but to be honest, I really don't know what to do with them. What I've found is actually having this stock creates some worry. I tend to watch it go up and down and that bugs me. I wish my dad hadn't left it to me because all I do is worry about it. For me, I just think I would rather play it safe and not worry about it.

How do you relate?

a. You've got to invest your money . . . quit watching it so much.

b. I say, if the roller coaster is making you sick, get off and ride something safer.

c. I agree with the fact that sometimes more money is not always better.

I Feel Your Pain

The stock market? Buddy, you gotta' be kidding me! After 73 years on planet Earth, and a lot of bad experiences in the stock market, here's how I would describe the whole Wall Street game: a sophisticated chain letter [sound of disgust]. *We all know the only people that really make money in the market are the ones selling the stuff and the big boys on Wall Street who are wheeling and dealing. Think about it . . . how many people you know really make much money over the long term? I don't know of any. The game is real easy for them: figure out a way to buy low, do something to drive up the stock prices, then, get out. In the meantime, simple people like me who don't have a clue what's going on, are left holding the bag. People are always referring to this as investing . . . heck, to me, if you don't know what you're doing with your money, you're a speculator, plain and simple. And one thing I'm not is a speculator."*

How do you relate?

a. There's no doubt that when it comes to investing, there have to be winners and losers. That's why I constantly preach knowing the market and the risks involved before jumping into it.

b. Based on his age and stage in life, I can relate to how he must feel about Wall Street.

c. This fellow needs to write a chain letter and send it to his favorite nursing home . . . I don't buy it.

The Thrill of the Chase

I have been very successful in business. The reason? I'm willing to take what I call "calculated" risks. For instance, my business today is worth well over $5,000,000; but, that is not really the whole point. I love the chase, I love the game, I love creating things and I am not afraid of losing my shirt. In fact, I've had to start over before. It's *really not that big of a deal as long as you believe in yourself and learn from your mistakes. But don't get me wrong; you'll never see me in the casinos. I'm not a gambler. I always research things very closely before ever investing in them. You've got to know how to read profit-and-loss statements and look at market trends very closely. If you take this approach, investing gets easier.*

How do you relate?

a. I like the part about him encouraging folks to understand financial statements and how to read profit and loss statements. I enjoy that kind of thing too.

b. I don't even know what a financial statement is, much less how to read one.

c. Why worry about money and risk? Stop worrying and go for the gusto, man!

The Tale of the Silver Dollar

I grew up during the Depression. I married young and stayed at home, taking care of the kids while my husband had a job as a bread truck driver. Every day, he would sell bread and bring home the cash from his employer—the profits of the day, if you will. If he ever had anything left over, we

*would turn it over at the bank into a silver dollar—
something that was widely used back then. We
had a goal: if we could save 500 silver dollars, we
would use that as a down payment on a house. After
several years, sure enough, we had the 500 silver
dollars and bought our first home. I learned a very
valuable lesson on savings . . . you don't have to
put it at risk to get things you want. In fact, during
the time we saved the 500 silver dollars, we didn't
even earn interest. But that didn't matter to us. We
were able to meet our goal and that was the most
important thing. So my thoughts, the key to being
successful financially, work hard, set a goal for
yourself, and save, save, save. Don't worry about
how much you make on your money, just save it.*

How do you relate?

a. Great story; obviously from a Depression-era
    person. Saving like that is so old-school though.
    I can't imagine *not* earning any interest on my
    money.

b. I don't trust banks. In 2009, over 95 banks went
    belly-up. What happens if some terrorist attack
    hits our soil again? I'm nervous and not sure
    what to do.

c. Let's forget the past, can we? Playing it safe is
    for old folks and sissies.

About the Author

Beginning his financial career in 1984, Tony Walker
has always considered himself a "contrarian"
of sorts (his favorite book as a child was Arty
the Smarty). Not one to follow the herd, Tony's
professional experience in the financial trenches—
forged over four different decades—has confirmed

much of what Tony has always believed: "that it's not about the money, but about people."

As the author of four books on retirement, as well as numerous appearances on Television, Tony Walker brings to the table his most innovative work to date, The 3 Personalities of Money®.

An expert on money, Tony is also an expert in the understanding of people and how they deal with money. He fully believes that the "one-size-fits-all" mentality pitched by the Financial World is the root of so many worries. While most people representing the Financial World seem preoccupied with how to make millions, Tony's mission in life is to simply to help millions.

A Registered Investment Advisor, he is a native and lifelong resident of the state of Kentucky. Besides a vast background in the study of finance, Tony has degrees in Psychology and Communication from Western Kentucky University. From 1998—2004, Tony hosted the TV show, "Your Money Matters" and for the past five years the featured weekly Retirement Specialist on NBC affiliate, "WAVE3 Listens Live" television show in Louisville Kentucky. Approaching 30 years of marriage to his high school sweetheart, Susan, together they enjoy their three children and four "personality-filled dogs."

List of Useful Websites and Publications

The following websites and articles are in no way to be reflected as an endorsement by Tony Walker. They are simply listed as possible options for research and education. Tony Walker accepts no responsibility for any information they might share with readers.

Resources for Savers

Website Resources for Savers

Safe Money Places: http://www.safemoneyplaces.com
BankRate.com: http://www.bankrate.com
Bankaholic.com: http://www.bankaholic.com
U.S. Treasury Direct: http://www.treasurydirect.gov
An Index Annuity Resource: http://www.indexannuity.org

Get Rich Slowly Blog: http://www.getrichslowly.
org/blog/
Mint.com: http://www.mint.com

Article Resources for Savers

Certificate of Deposits vs. Treasury Bills:
http://www.ehow.com/about_5371895_certifcate-
deposits-vs-treasury-bills.html

Ultimate guide to retirement: Annuities: http://
money.cnn.com/retirement/ guide/Annuities/

Which Places are Safe?
http://www.safemoneyplaces.com/ places.htm
How to be Your Own Financial Regulator:
http://finance.yahoo.com/expert/ article/
moneyhappy/228606

Investopedia: How to Calculate Taxable Equivalent
Yield for Municipal Bonds:
http://www.ehowcom/how_4823112_taxable-
equivalent-yield-municipal-bonds.html

Investopedia: The Basics of Municipal Bonds:
http://www.investopedia.com/articles/
bonds/05/022805.asp?viewed=1

Treasury Direct: Learn How to Purchase Treasury
Securities:

http://www.treasurydirect.gov/indiv/myaccount/
myaccount.htm

Life Insurance Buyer's Guide:
http://www.naic.org/documents/consumer_guide_
life.pdf

Resources for Investors:

Website Resources for Investors:

The Motley Fool: http://www.fool.com
Investopedia: A Forbes Digital Company: http://www.
investopedia.com/
Global Value Investing: http://www.numeraire.com/
invest.htm
Yahoo: Finance: http://finance.yahoo.com/
MarketWatch: http://www.marketwatch.com/
CNBC: http://www.cnbc.com
U.S. Securities and Exchange Commission: http://
www.sec.gov/
U.S. Small Business Administration and Investment
Division: http://www.sba.gov/

Article Resources for Investors:

Investopedia: Investing Tutorials—Basics
http://www.investopedia.com/ university/
buildingblocks.asp

Motley Fool: Mutual Funds—Expense Ratio
http://www.fool.com/school/mutualfunds/costs/
ratios.htm

SEC.gov: Mutual Fund Prospectus, Tips for
Reading One
http://www.sec.gov/answers/mfprospectustips.htm

MSNBC.com: "I want to invest, but I'm clueless
about stocks"
http://www.msnbc.com/id/9842790/

EHow.com: "How to Pick a Stock to Invest In"
http://www.ehow.com/how_6327707_
pick-stock-invest.html

EHow.com: "What Are the Differences Between
Stocks and Bonds?" http://www.ehow.com/
about_5270791_differences-between-stocks-bonds.
html.

MSNBC.com: Real Estate Investing
http://articles.moneycentral.msn.com/Investing/
RealEstate/RealEstate.aspx

U.S. Small Business Administration and Investment
Division: Seeking SBIC Financing for your Small
Business
http://www.sba.gov/aboutsba/sbaprogrms/inv/est/
INV_SBIC_FINANCING.html

Resources for Speculators

Website Resources for Speculators:

Forex Currency Trading: http://forex.com/pages/
land-international.html
Active Trader Magazine: http://www.
activetradermag.com/
Foreclosure Real Estate Listings: http://www.
realtytrac.com
Interactive Brokers: http://www.interactivebrokers.
com/ ibg/main.php
Direct Trade Futures: http://www.dtfutures.com
History of Gold and Silver: http://www.
historyofgoldandsilver. org/
Direxion Funds: http://www.direxionfunds.com/

Article Resources for Speculators:

EHow.com: "How to Buy Commodities Online"
http://www.ehow.com/how_5094988_
buy-commodities-online.html

A Short Course introducing Commodity Markets
& Futures Trading http://futures.tradingcharts.com/
tafm/

EHow.com: "How to invest in Precious Metals"
http://www.ehow.com/how_109625_
invest-precious-metals.html.

WSJ.com: "How to Buy a Foreclosed Home"
http://online.wsj.com/article/
SB121640621223565845.html.www.ETFvirtual.
com

Marketwatch.com: "How to buy . . . options"
http://www.marketwatch.com/story/how-to-buy
options

The History of Gold www.nmo.org/pdf/gold/
gold_history. pdf

EHow.com: "How to Invest in an Oil or Gas Well &
Investing in Oil Exploration."
http://www.ehow.com/how_4447947_gas-well-
investing-oil-exploration.html